MW01700827

PRESENCE PRESENTS

The Gift Book

Leanne Dalderis
and
Maynard Dalderis

Cover and Layout
Kelly Hewkin, IntuitiveGraphicDesign.com

Cover Artwork
Jennifer Blair is a noted Calgary artist. For Jennifer, art is an intense physical, emotional and spiritual discipline that brings us in touch with our inner reality.

Presence Presents: The Gift Book
ISBN 978-0-921154-20-4

Leanne Dalderis and Maynard Dalderis

Publisher
Guideline Productions Inc.
Calgary, Alberta, Canada
e| dalderis@vitagenics.ca
w| www.livingwithguidance.ca

Acknowledgements

We gratefully acknowledge all those who continually asked us, "When are you going to publish these gifts?", without you this would still be a manuscript.

We acknowledge each one of you in our lives —you truly are the gift.

We acknowledge God and all the gifts that are given—we are in awe.

Table of Contents

OPENING TO THE GIFTS

WHAT ARE THE GIFTS?

The gifts were given to us, appropriately enough, during the Christmas of 1989. We had, and still have, a group that meets every Wednesday night, and we wanted to give each of them some sort of gift to celebrate the essence of Christmas. We were already somewhat cynical with the gift giving process that occurs during the Christmas season. But still, there was a strong desire to give something that would share what was in our hearts; that would share the depth of our feeling of gratitude for each person that had come to share and open in our group.

And so, we tried to look for things—some little token that would express the true spirit of giving; that would express our feeling of connection. But, things cost money and while we were not adverse to spending money, the issue still became—how much, what sort of items, how big, how little, how meaningful? We soon found ourselves enmeshed in the very commotions we found so jading with the whole holiday season. We wanted to give—but what would have any meaning at all?

Our guidance, sensing our weariness and confusion, asked us to begin sharing what was in our hearts, what attributes, feelings, or blessing would we wish each member to receive. These, they said, were gifts.

We thought about it for a while and realized we wished each person who came to our home to receive the gift of Peace—how appropriate that felt, especially at Christmas time. We wished to give the gift of Love, the gift of Joy, and again, for Christmas time, the gift of an extended family. We wished to give the gift of never having to walk alone, the gift of connection, and the gift of Sharing.

We began to realize that the very gifts we wanted to give were the gifts we were most wanting to receive in our lives. It became easier to know what we wanted to give when we looked into our own hearts and got in touch with our own asking.

Soon we had about 110 gifts written down—all the gifts you will find in this book. We were asked to write each gift on a separate piece of paper and simply to ask each person to pick a gift out of the deck we had written. Something felt complete with this giving and we were excited to share the gift of all the Gifts with the group on Christmas Eve. We wondered how the group would accept our gifts, but needn't have worried—it turned out to be one of the most joyful and opening meetings we had, or ever since experienced. You see, we opened our true gifts.

As Maynard went around the circle handing out the gifts, the room seemed to get brighter and brighter. People were laughing, crying, touched, puzzled, and amazed at the accuracy of the gifts each had chosen. The beauty of the gifts was that if one person liked the gift another had chosen, they could have the same gift too. Not only was there enough to go around, each gift became everyone else's. It was, for us, a very moving evening and with each present, we felt the Presence of God. For this we finally understood—the presents we gave and wanted to receive were all gifts of God. That's why they had so much meaning for us—they connected us with His Presence.

We really can't explain the gifts, even today. To us, they are simply a reminder to let God be in charge of our lives in a 110 different ways. They are a reminder of what God gives to us just for the asking. They are a reminder that the gifts are already open and only await our willingness to receive them. They are a reminder that we don't have to become deserving of them—we are given them freely, unconditionally, and continually. They remind us of what is in our hearts, of what is in the hearts of others and of what is in God. They are a reminder of His Presence that is always with us.

We can't explain them—they are unconditional. They are ours to give with our asking, but they are not ours to control. They are God given gifts.

Since that meeting we have shared the gifts, asked for the gifts and learned about the gifts. Quite often in groups of people we know, and in groups where we don't know anyone, Maynard will pass out the gifts. He will say, "Pick a card and see what the universe has in store for you." He gets varied reactions—surprise, suspicion, delight, wonder. But each person who sees their gift seems touched in some way, for they always ask—can I keep it? and the answer is always, "Yes."

We wish to share the gifts with you, for with these gifts, the more gifts you ask for, receive, and share, the more there is for everyone and the more we realize the gift that each one of us is, and the gift that God is.

May you receive these gifts with all our blessings and may the spirit of Christmas be in your hearts each moment of each and every day.

--Leanne and Maynard Dalderis

OPENING TO GOD'S GIFTS

When we try to attain those gifts, which we think would make us happy, we cannot be open to God's gifts.

Each day we climb onto our hamster wheel and race after what we think will make us happy. We do not climb down long enough to receive the happiness of God's gifts.

If we really, honestly, look at our goals, they are not sought for the happiness they bring—they are sought to relieve the desperate feeling inside of us. This is the stuff of addictions. This is the difference between "my will" and "Thy Will."

We are not pursuing happiness, we are pursuing what we think will make us happy—there is a vast difference between the two.

Our goals are always to relieve the desperation we feel from our separation with our Higher Power. Our goals, then, are sought to relieve, avoid, and to try to fill our emptiness. Really, it is not release from what we focus on in recovery—it is our Higher Power's Will for us, which ultimately is the very happiness we seek.

Trying to relieve the separation from our Higher Power is our search and our addiction.

If we are seeking to tell the difference between our will and God's Will, it is very simple: our will, will be an eternal attempt to relieve some desperation. God's Will, will be happiness in the moment while seeing events unfold in the most appropriate way.

We will find ourselves experiencing happiness, not because of what we are doing, but because of our being. We will see people happy no matter what they are doing, for they know they are in touch with God's gifts. They are off of the hamster wheel and into the flow.

That is why the pursuit of our goals puts us on the hamster wheel—these goals can never be fulfilled—they are empty.

Gratification and Gratitude are totally contradictory.

Gratitude is the bond that connects us—gratification is the knife that severs us. This does not make gratification wrong—it only makes us desperate.

Yes, we have the power to obtain all our goals. We have the power to focus on and obtain everything we set out to do. But having obtained these things will not lessen the desperation they are supposed to replace—they will only increase it.

When we pray only for the knowledge of God's Will for us and His Power to carry it out, we are no longer in pursuit of our goals. Indeed we are no longer in pursuit of happiness—for we have found it. It has been given.

God's Will for us:

> *"Please accept all of My Gifts I would lovingly give to you and share them with each other."*

GIFT IDEAS

The gifts we receive we cannot help but give away—it is inherent in the gift.

Each gift contains all other gifts—it can be no other way. If you have the gift of Trust, you will also have the gift of Choice. If you have the gift of Connection, you will also have the gift of Awareness.

The gift of Choice is not a gift of judgment, it is a gift to always choose what is for everyone's well-being—what is for everyone's peace and healing.

You may search in many different directions, but if you ask for Truth, no matter where you seek, Truth will bring you to the Oneness within all things.

In all gifts it is the thought that counts—the One Thought.

Gifts are not given to us so we may do it—gifts are the doing.

Each gift will not be a gift to hold on to; it will be a gift to let go of.

IN THE BEGINNING

Beginning is not an end; it is a beginning. With some annoyance you say: "Very profound!" We say you miss the point, for you still have beginning confused with ending.

Let us show you. You think that to begin you must be committed to whatever you begin. But commitment only narrows down your choice to one way of doing things. Thus, you see beginning as an end of choice. You see beginning as a point where you shut out all other solutions in order to begin. You see beginning as a point where you can no longer make any mistakes. It is the end, then, of freedom, for you no longer have the freedom to begin without judgment. You are not allowed to do anything "wrong".

Your beginning is an end to all solutions because you have determined that you can only follow one solution. Your beginning, then, has a closure. It is the beginning of the end.

So, that is why we say: beginning is not an end; it is a beginning.

Beginning is still having choice. Beginning is opening to all solutions each moment. Beginning is being able to admit our mistakes without judgment so that these too may be used for our healing on our journey. Beginning allows freedom. We simply cannot begin without the gift of choice being with that beginning. It is the end of nothing—it is the beginning.

We begin with simplicity.

We begin with solutions that are constantly given.

We begin with ease.

We begin with opening.

We begin wherever we happen to be.

We begin with the beginning.

We begin with freedom.

We begin with lightness.

We begin with the willingness to be willing.

We begin with completeness.

We begin with all awareness.

We begin with God being our Beginning.

THE GIFTS

THE GIFT OF A LOVING HEART

We have tried hard to love, but we did not know how. We found that we had "love" for some people, but not for others. We found that even with those we thought we loved, there were times when we wished to get rid of them—we even thought we hated them.

There was much guilt for the hatred we felt and there was much fear that what we did love would soon turn to hatred or disillusionment. We tried to maintain love, and were exhausted. We tried to prove our love, and became desperate. We felt guilty at our inability to keep and maintain a loving heart. We did things to those we were supposed to love, that we judged that someone with a caring heart would not do.

We knew we were supposed to love, but we did not know how. We covered our lack of a loving heart with much pretence and well-meaning actions. We did not admit we didn't know how to care.

> **We cannot make ourselves loving. A loving heart is a gift. The ability to love and care is a gift. It does not matter how we try to be loving or what we do to be loving—a loving heart is a gift. There is nothing to make up to anyone for our lack of a loving heart. It is a gift that is given to us. It is a gift of our**

> **Higher Power's Heart. It is with His Love that we may Love. It is with His Heart that we may care. It is with the gift of a loving heart that all our guilt for not knowing how to care is washed away.**

It is with the gift of a loving heart that we may see love with everyone and exclude no one from its presence. It is with the gift of a loving heart that we are there for each other at the most appropriate place and time.

This gift knows no limits nor makes any judgments. We cannot lose this gift; it is given each time we remember to ask for God's gift of a loving heart.

THE GIFT OF ACCEPTANCE

We have thought that acceptance meant that we had to be satisfied with pain, misery, and desperation. We thought acceptance meant being stuck with our circumstances and having to like it. For these reasons, many of us resisted acceptance with all our being, for acceptance seemed to be giving in to what was causing us so much pain and anguish.

But the gift of acceptance is not giving in to, nor giving up on; it is finally seeing that what we give to our Higher Power for healing will always be resolved for everyone's well-being. The gift of acceptance, then, is the realization that there is another way beyond what seems to be happening to us. Acceptance isn't to condone where we are; it is to admit where we are without having to judge it or condemn it.

The gift of acceptance is the key to going beyond whatever confronts us, for whatever we resist we do not release and a solution cannot be given. The gift of acceptance would have us admit where we are in order to go beyond where we are. We accept without judgment that we perceive a situation a certain way, and we accept that another way, another solution, will always be given by our Higher Power. We accept that all we need do is ask for our Higher Power's solution. We even accept our doubts so that they may have answers.

The gift of acceptance is a gift that comes totally without judgment, totally without guilt, and totally without fear. The gift of acceptance is our Higher Power's gift of another way. We accept that we too may have love, peace, and happiness in our lives. We accept there will be a loving and healing solution to our conflicts. We accept ease and well-being. We accept God's Will for us because that Will allows for all the expression of our being.

The gift of acceptance is simply the admittance that our will no longer works, and with this admittance is the gift that there will always be an answer that will heal all conflicts, circumstances, and all else we have made.

THE GIFT OF ACCEPTING GOD'S GIFTS NOW

There is a very wise saying, which we have perhaps heard many times. Very simply it says: "One day at a time." We would even make it more specific: "One moment at a time." For you see, we can only accept God's gifts now—just for today—just for this moment.

We often wish to be in charge of our security. We wish to make sure we do not experience old feelings of pain and fear again. We do not wish to experience feelings of helplessness and despair. We wish to secure the future and make it a place where fear and want cannot enter. So attached are we to our security that we feel very insecure, indeed, in case anyone or anything may threaten it. We are consumed with protecting the future. We become very serious and desperate to do all those things that will assure our future security.

But we have forgotten one thing—we have forgotten to accept, just for today, all of God's wonderous gifts. We have forgotten to accept the gift of all being taken care of "just for today", "just for this moment"—NOW.

When we take charge of our security, or of how the future should be, we close ourselves off to our Higher Power's wisdom and appropriateness. We begin to make conditions: "I will be happy when I know I will have enough money for many years to come. I will feel safe when my house is paid for. I will be able to let in joy when my career is firmly established. I will be able to have peace when I am finally through looking at and releasing my past. I will feel that all is taken care of when I figure out how to keep and maintain what I already have. I will be happy when I know I will be happy down the road. I will feel safe when I finally find the right people and the right connections and when I know those connections will be maintained. I can't accept God's gifts until..."

We have decided we will be happy when; we have not seen we can choose to receive that gift—now.

The gift of accepting God's gifts Now is simply a realization that we need control nothing in order to receive the gifts this very moment. We may receive the gifts—just for today. And in receiving them just for today—receive them always. For it is one day at a time that they are given to us. We can put our happiness on hold. We can put our feeling supported and taken care of on hold, or we may ask for this gift—now.

If we say: "I'll choose happiness when... I'll choose Ease and peace when..." then the gifts will always be just out of our reach. But, if just for each day, we ask for the gift of appropriateness in all that we do; if just for today we ask for the gift of Enthusiasm, the gift of Motivation in whatever it is we wish to accomplish, then these gifts are ours instantly.

It is by being present that we receive all gifts. We can only be taken care of—now. We can truly only be happy—now. And by accepting God's gifts now, we are in touch with the truth of each moment unfolding continually and endlessly before us.

THE GIFT OF ACCOMPLISHMENT

It is by being centered that all things are accomplished. It is by choosing to be with our Higher Power that each step of our journey is accomplished. It is by being in the moment that what is appropriate is always accomplished.

It has seemed that certain things had to be accomplished before we could have peace, happiness or even healing. But truly, it is only when we come from peace that any true and lasting accomplishment takes place.

The gift of accomplishment is the gift of being in touch with our Higher Power Whose Will accomplishes everything.

Accomplishment has seemed to take place outside of ourselves, but in reality, it is an inside job. When we are centered and at peace, we join in a flow that is connected to all things. From this center, beginnings are made, appropriate connections take place, and the journey unfolds with gratitude and wonder for the gifts that each step brings.

The gift of Accomplishment is the gift of beginning with our Higher Power and what is accomplished is healing from all our pain and sorrow.

The gift of Accomplishment is truly the gift of God's Will for us:

> *"Thy Accomplishment be done."*

Accomplishment is not a condition on peace. It is not something we must prove, it is not something we must fulfill in order to be deserving or feel worthy. It is a gift that is given to us where we see miracles accomplished when we let our Source be the accomplishment. It is not a quota we must fulfill. It is not a list we must complete. It is not an expectation to live up to.

It is truly the gift of having our desperate commotions to "accomplish something" replaced with the accomplishment that heals relationships, that brings people together in support and understanding, that finds solutions, that reveals another way, that includes everyone's well-being. And what is accomplished is a solution that includes everyone in its love, in its care, and in its direction.

The gift of Accomplishment is the gift of being at Home, the moment we choose the peace, the solution of our Higher Power.

What greater accomplishment is there than to see the love that we are?

What greater accomplishment is there than to see the innocence of each other?

What greater accomplishment is there than to have respect for all beings?

What greater accomplishment is there than to feel totally alive and joyous?

What greater accomplishment is there than to see forgiveness where there has been resentment and fear?

What greater accomplishment is there than to feel the peace of each moment?

What greater accomplishment is there than to let God be our Accomplishment?

THE GIFT OF ADMITTANCE

So often we see admittance as confession. We have to "admit" or confess our sins in order to feel guilty about them. With this idea about admittance, the gift of Admittance does not seem to be a gift at all. This only seems to open us to more shame, guilt, and blame.

But truly, admittance is letting in. We admit in order to let in more light. We admit in order to let in healing. We admit in order to let in life itself. We admit in order to let in our Higher Power. In other words, we admit One Who can set us free from all pain and conflict that we experience.

The gift of Admittance is a gift that lets in, in order to heal. The whole point of this gift is that when we finally admit, we will release our guilt in order to admit innocence. We will admit our weaknesses in order to release them and to let in our strength. We will admit our shame so it may be cleansed and so we may admit our true worth. We admit in order to let in. We do not admit in order to find ourselves guilty.

The gift of Admittance lets in all other gifts. It is literally like carrying a ticket that says "admit one" to all joy, to all support; admit one to be included in all things caring, nurturing, and healing.

We admit whatever we have done "wrong" in order to be given another way. We do not admit our wrongs to be judged and condemned. We admit them so they may be gently corrected and so we may find Peace.

We admit Love into our lives. We admit Happiness. We admit Freedom. Our lives have been filled with what we would hide. The gift of Admittance is the light that we would shine on our darkness to have it disappear.

The gift of Admittance is the ability to let in, so everyone may see us beyond our mistakes, beyond our pettiness, beyond our craziness, and beyond our fears.

The gift of Admittance is the gift of letting ourselves be seen, of admitting others in order to see our worth, and our innocence.

We admit One Who has all power. We admit One Who forgives and accepts. We admit One that brings Love and Light. We admit One to dissolve all we have made. We admit our Higher and Innermost Power.

THE GIFT OF ALL BEING TAKEN CARE OF

We are full of many cares at times. At times we are so full of cares that we cease to care about anyone or anything. Our shoulders carry many burdens and we feel there are countless problems to be faced and resolved. We are full of cares but we do not experience caring.

Finally handing everything over to our Higher Power will give us the gift of all being taken care of. For whatever we turn over to our Higher Power can then be healed and resolved. It is what we hang on to that becomes a care; it is what we give over that becomes taken care of.

This gift removes all burdens from our shoulders. We are in God's Care now and it is with His Care that we both receive caring and have this gift to give. With this gift we care about life again; we care about honesty and respect; we care about others and pass on this gift of caring in all we do.

Each problem we give our Higher Power is taken care of and in return we receive our Higher Power's Care. The only limit to this gift is our insistence that there is still some area or problem that cannot be given to our Higher Power. In these areas we do not experience the gift of God's Care and indeed it will seem as though no one cares.

The more we are willing to give our Higher Power all our cares, the more we will experience the gift of all being taken care of.

THE GIFT OF ALL MY MIRRORS

We are not always comfortable around mirrors, for mirrors faithfully reflect exactly where we are and precisely where we are coming from. Each mirror is a true reflection of our inner state of mind. In each mirror we see ourselves reflected back. Some mirrors we find pleasant to look into. They reflect that part of ourselves which is considerate, helpful, and aware. But there are those mirrors we dislike most intensely, for they reflect faithfully our controls and all our defects of character. These mirrors we wish to avoid. And if we cannot avoid them, we spend time trying to fix our mirrors, desperately hoping that this would be the solution to our discomfort of what we see reflected.

But each and every one of our mirrors is a gift—the gift of all our mirrors. Whatever judgment that we need to let go of, the mirrors will show us in minute detail. In each mirror that we see anger, distrust, deceit or fear, we see ourselves and what is in our hearts. This is indeed a gift for we are not required to judge what we see, we are only asked to give these defects of character over to a loving God in order for Him to release them. By ourselves, we cannot see what needs to be healed in our lives, but what we see in our mirrors is precisely what we need to let go of.

And ultimately, the gift of all our mirrors will reflect back truly who we are, in all our innocence, all our love, all our consideration, and all our connection with our Higher Power. Each mirror is a gift, for beyond what we judge in our mirror we will see ourselves, complete, whole, and totally forgiven.

> *"Mirror, mirror, just like me...*
> *You are the one to set me free."*

THE GIFT OF AN EXTENDED FAMILY

We have not always felt that we "fit" or belonged in our own families. We have usually felt a stranger amongst our relatives. We either tried to fit in so much that we lost touch with who we were, or we resisted and rebelled so much that we never let ourselves get close to anyone.

Some of us tried to hide what was happening in our families. Others of us sought to expose it. Some of us sought to please, and when that did not work, we sought to anger and disturb. Some sought to achieve impossible goals. Some of us never lived up to our abilities. Some of us sought destruction. All of us sought love and attention the only way we knew how. We sought to be with the members of our family and when we could not, when they did not know how to let us, we pushed them away and tried to push them out of our lives.

We could not always speak what was in our hearts to those in our family. Sometimes they wished us to be what we were not; they wished us to conform to their ideals and expectations.

Sometimes there were rivalries and jealousies that we did not understand. Sometimes there were old hurts and resentments that we could not forgive—old disappointments in times when we were let down, cut off, or abandoned.

Always, did we wish to be heard and seen for who we truly were. We simply wished to be loved and accepted. We wanted to know we were doing okay, no matter what happened. We wanted the members of our family to appreciate us and see our worth. We wished them to allow us to be.

The gift of an extended family gives a gift that goes far beyond our family of origin. It gives us the family that we have always longed for—a family of support and caring. A family of openness and honesty. A family of integrity and respect. A family of understanding and sharing. A family where we can share our pain and joy, our hopes and fears, our mistakes and our solutions. A family we can always call upon. A family we love to come home to. A family that watches and encourages our steps of freedom and discovery. A family filled with love and with acceptance for who we are. A family of laughter and joy. A family where our heart can open and extend its love and all the gifts we hold inside. A family where we can be. A family given by our Higher Power.

This is the family our Higher Power would give us when we ask for this gift. And the beauty of this family is that it can be found anywhere.

No longer are we limited by trying to find happiness, worth and freedom in our family of origin.

The gift of an extended family is a gift that brings us home to ourselves. It teaches us that we can allow ourselves to be. We can allow ourselves to join with others. We can allow ourselves to express what is in our innermost heart; what is for our well-being. We can allow ourselves to receive love and forgiveness. We can come home to our Higher Power. We can come home to our true family.

With the gift of an extended family, our Higher Power becomes the connection that heals all separation. Our Higher Power becomes the bridge that reaches each of us so we can finally truly see and hear each other. Our Higher Power becomes the love that enfolds the family and releases it from all its pain and dis-ease.

The gift of an extended family is a gift that truly connects us with everyone—there is truly no one we are not a part of. There is no one we cannot feel at home with. Each person we meet becomes a gift of sharing and opening. Each heart becomes a recognition of ourselves. In each encounter we find a soul that our Higher Power is expressing through.

Our family becomes an inclusion of all people, for there is no one in whom we do not find ourselves and in whom we do not find our answers. We do not have to be alone—we are reconnected with ourselves. We are reconnected with our family, and we are reconnected with all others. There is no us and them, there is only—"There go I".

And with this gift, we find healing with our family of origin. We have a limitless, supportive family to guide us in releasing old hurts, resentments and feelings of disconnection that we still carry from this family. We begin to realize, with this gift, that each member of our family wishes the same thing—they, too, wish love and acceptance. They, too, are afraid of rejection and do not feel worthy. They, too, wish to be connected and part of something they are able to express freely within. They, too, have not felt loved and appreciated—they, too, have not known how to show love, to show feelings, to show themselves. With the gift of an extended family, we are reunited with the family of our childhood in forgiveness, in honesty and in healing.

The family of our childhood, and the family that comes with the gift of an extended family become one family, one heart. The gift of an extended family is the gift that our Higher Power brings us each time we say, "Please show me the innocence in this person." We are at home with ourselves, we are at home with each other, we are all at home in our Higher Power.

THE GIFT OF ANOTHER WAY

In all our confusion and in all our despair, we have not seen that there might be another way. We have only seen that we are stuck and that there appears to be no solution to the pain and separation that surrounds us.

The gift of another way is a way out of hell, for it says: "There is nothing that cannot be healed; there is nothing that cannot be resolved; there is no solution that cannot be found; there is no darkness that cannot be brought to light; there is nothing that cannot be forgiven; there is no experience that cannot be released; there is no fear that cannot be seen through."

The gift of another way is the gift of our Higher Power's way. The whole point is: we do not know the way—it is a gift that is given. We do not have to know the way; it is a gift that says: "With God there is always another way of healing and of release."

The gift of another way is truly the gift of all other gifts, for our way has only brought pain and fear. With the gift of our Higher Power's way, we receive the way of Love, the way of Peace, the way of Understanding, the way of Answers and Solutions.

We don't have to know the way or find the way. We don't have to see the way. We don't have to understand the way. We don't have to make the way. We don't have to prepare for the way. This is the gift that simply says: "To all your problems and difficulties there is another way."

The simple willingness to consider another way is the gift. A little willingness in the midst of our tension and confusion, in the midst of our conflict and control is enough to allow this gift to enter.

From all our despair, there is another way. From all our fear and hatred, there is another way. From all our crazy patterns, there is another way. From all our misunderstanding and separation, there is another way. From everything we have ever made or done, there is another way. Are we willing to ask for the gift of another way?

When we truly see the controls we are using, it is not to blame or judge ourselves. It is to have the opportunity to see there is another way.

When we finally admit all the grievances we have been holding, all the resentments, it is not for us to feel guilty. It is for us to see that with a sense of real-ease—there is another way. Another way is always given—we need only ask for this gift.

THE GIFT OF APPRECIATION

We have not known how to really appreciate life. We have not known how to appreciate what we already had, nor were we able to appreciate that we already had it. We were not able to appreciate those who were in our lives, but most of all we were not able to appreciate who we were and what we had to give. So busy had we been pursuing endless goals that never brought fulfillment that there was a definite lack of appreciation in our lives.

The gift of Appreciation allows us to truly appreciate simplicity in our lives. It shows us we can appreciate peace and happiness. The gift of Appreciation shows us we can be happy with the simple joy of a moment. With this gift we begin to appreciate another way that our Higher Power always gives us. We begin to appreciate there is always a solution. We begin to appreciate simple things and simple gifts.

With this gift we are able to appreciate the gifts that are ours. We are able to appreciate what others have to offer and we are able to appreciate our own life and the gifts we have to give. With this gift we are able to appreciate life. We are able to open up to all the joys of living and of expression—we appreciate there is another way. With this gift we are able to let in all gifts with true appreciation of their value to us and to others.

With appreciation things appreciate as more and more their value is revealed to us.

THE GIFT OF APPROPRIATENESS

We have been so afraid of doing the wrong thing. We have been afraid of saying the wrong thing, choosing the wrong path, being with the wrong person. So convinced were we at times that we were wrong, that there was something wrong with us, that we believed that anything we did could not help but be wrong.

Much of our lives have been centered around avoidance of doing the wrong thing. We have lived in fear that the decisions we make will be wrong for us. We have lived in fear that the choices we make may be the wrong ones and bring irrevocable harm to ourselves or someone else.

Sometimes each decision we make feels somehow wrong. If we decide one way—that feels wrong. If we decide another way—that also feels wrong. Very seldom does a decision feel "right".

The gift of appropriateness, first of all, recognizes that a child of God can do no wrong. This does not mean that we cannot make mistakes; it simply means that our mistakes do not make our being wrong.

Truly, the gift of appropriateness is allowing our Higher Power to use everything for healing and in fact to be the healing. It is the admittance that we, by ourselves, cannot know what is appropriate. It is the recognition that our Higher Power is the appropriateness within us..."What is the appropriateness of Thy Will?"

The gift of appropriateness is the gift of coming from the innocence and integrity of our being and having that innocence and integrity reflected in all that we do. We are all children of God and in this recognition will all that we do be appropriate.

All of God's gifts are most appropriate. When in doubt about what to give, ask for the appropriateness of God's gifts.

THE GIFT OF BEAUTY

Many of us do not relate to this gift. We can see how nature may be beautiful. We may even recognize the appearance of beauty in certain people. In most others, we do not see any beauty and find this concept, this gift, difficult to see. But even more difficult is seeing the beauty within ourselves. We do not see ourselves as beautiful or containing the gift of Beauty. We are somewhat embarrassed when we pull the gift of beauty, for in most cases the very last thing we see ourselves as is beautiful.

Beauty, to us, is like the old adage—"Beauty is only skin deep." We deny any connection of beauty with ourselves and are highly suspicious of anyone that would call us beautiful.

Truly, the beauty we speak of is not skin deep. It is not the beauty of appearance or the beauty that fades and falls away. We speak of the beauty of a heart willing to open. We speak of the beauty of someone willing to be all they can be. We speak of the beauty of honesty beyond all fear of being seen. We speak of the beauty of a heart sharing what is within it.

We speak of a beauty that is heart deep and heart felt. There is nothing more beautiful than the innocence of the child within us all. There is nothing more beautiful than a soul willing to go beyond its darkest beliefs and conclusions to the light of its true being.

We speak of the beauty of admittance. We speak of the beauty of kindness and compassion. We speak of the beauty of loving thoughts and actions. We speak of the beauty of forgiveness and the beauty of the soul that shines forth when we truly let go and let forgiveness bring the beauty back into our lives. We speak of the beauty of recognizing ourselves in the heart of another. There is nothing more beautiful than this connection.

We speak of the beauty of understanding. We speak of the beauty of faith. And what makes each of us beautiful is the light of our Higher Power shining forth in each one of us. There is no one who is not beautiful in the light of God's Vision. There is no one who is not beautiful in the light of their radiant innocence and oneness.

Yes, there is much beauty, not in appearance, but in spirit. For it is the spirit that lights the countenance with the beauty so pure and real that we will see our beauty reflected in the eyes and hearts of others.

Yes, there is much beauty in each of God's gifts. The Light of God is the beauty. The heart of God is what is beautiful. We invite you to embrace and express the beauty that is within you and all around you.

THE GIFT OF BEGINNING—LET US BEGIN

You have strange ways of beginning. You have certain conditions on your beginning. Beginning means many different things to many different people.

Beginning to some means bringing in all the options before they can start. In other words, they cannot do anything until the overall picture is known. This is called beginning. The problem with this beginning is that the overall picture becomes the condition that must be fulfilled before anything can be started. Consequently, they are often too busy bringing everything in to begin.

Other beginnings are much different. Some begin by shutting everything out in order to accomplish the task at hand. They begin, then, by keeping out everything except what they are doing. The problem with this beginning is that it takes much energy to keep out everything and it does not allow for any support or alternate solutions. Keeping out becomes a condition on being able to begin.

Let's look at a solution or a beginning that has no conditions. We begin with first things first, while allowing all else into our awareness. This is much different than having to bring things in or keep things out. We open to or allow our Higher Power to show us all solutions and to give us the gift of choice so that we may begin what is needed to be done immediately.

When we allow in and begin with first things first, there is a natural unfoldment where everything is done in its appropriate time and space. This unfoldment will even take us beyond time and place to be in the moment.

Our Higher Power is in charge of our opening and our allowing. We begin with first things first, while having this allowance flow into our lives.

All else becomes a condition on our beginning. We may begin knowing there will be a natural unfoldment taking place. We may begin with our Higher Power in charge of our beginning. We may begin by giving up any conditions on beginning. We simply begin by doing that which is brought before us. We begin with Joy and we begin with our Higher Power in charge of what is in front of us and what is all around us. We begin with another way.

THE GIFT OF BEING

Truly, what is beyond all our controls is simply the gift of Being. We have lost sight of the value of this gift, for always have we been taught: "You have to be something." It was never good enough simply to be who we were. Indeed, simply being, the power of simply being, has been forgotten. Most of us do not know how to be. We don't know how to be who we are, where we are, wherever we are coming from, at Peace, in the moment...and so on.

The power of Being is an incredible gift, for ultimately that is the gift of Being with God. We have our being in God and instead of losing our being by letting God into our lives, we will find our being supported in all its creativity, expression, and the awareness of our very soul of being.

The gift of Being is a gift where we are totally without judgment—we are too busy being.

In one way or another, all our pain, all our conflict, all our unhappiness and all our insanity has been a result of being unable to be, of being detached from our very being or essence.

We are starting to see, it is not what we do that is important—it is where we come from. We are speaking here of being. It has always seemed before that we must do in order to be. But we find this is backwards, and in fact is quite impossible. The spirit of our Being—that center of Being with God; that gift of Being in touch with who we truly are; that great value of our Being—is the only true place to come from. If we have to do something before we can be, we are out of touch with both—the Being that our Higher Power is and the doing that this Being expresses.

Being is where we must begin. Seeing another Being is where we must start.

The gift of Being is finally being in touch with that center of Peace within, with that Sanity within, with that Strength and Divinity within, no matter what insanities have been or are in our lives.

When we come from our Being, from innocence, from the gifts we have to offer—the doing is automatic and comes from our "well"-spring of Being.

The gift of Being requires no conditions from us. It does not require that we be or do anything in order to be loved. The gift of Being allows us simply to come from our Being and in that Being will all our doing be a reflection of strength, direction, and power.

Being with God allows us to do what is His Will for us. In this there is no separation between Being and doing, for doing will be an extension of our Being in everything that we do.

Be still and know that I Am your Being.

Be still and know that this Being is innocent and pure.

Be still and know that this Being will reflect Love and Light in whatever is done.

My Will is your Being.

My Will is not to overwhelm or destroy your Being. It is to put you in touch with it.

My Being is your Being and all others' Being.

Be still and ask for the gift of Being, for this Being will be the doing.

Be still and be in My Peace, and be in My Care—this will be Our doing.

Thy Being be done.

Spirit is the Being—religion is the form or the doing. If you put the form or the doing first, you will lose the Spirit and be left with an empty form.

But, if you put Being first—the Spirit of Being with your Higher Power, then the doing will be guided by this Spirit and in Truth will become One with it.

There really is no difference between Being and doing. Some people confusedly think that Being does not require any doing. But seen truly, when we are coming from our Being, it is the most natural thing to extend this and share it—this is the doing. We extend that which we would keep. We share that which we would be.

Again, if we put doing first, we become disconnected from our Source or our Being. This is the separation we feel anytime we put doing first—it will appear that Being and doing are quite separate.

But coming from being, this true God-given gift of Being, we will automatically be inspired to share this gift, extend this gift, express this gift, remember this gift, and to give this gift. We will see this gift in others, and in our seeing, they will see. We will see this gift in ourselves and be a light to many. Still others will see this gift in us and this will be our remembrance, this will be our call to Be. We are all at one in our Being. And this indeed will be the doing of "Thy Will be done."

THE GIFT OF BEING ABLE TO DOUBT AND QUESTION

As children, we were often told—"Don't question, just do it!" We were asked to believe in a God that we could not doubt or question and we were told that to do so would be sacrilege and met with great punishment. We were taught not to question our parents—"Do as I say not as I do!" We were taught not to question our teachers—they knew what was best for us. We were taught not to question authority. We were not able to doubt and question the religious beliefs we were taught and the books that taught them to us. We were not able to doubt and question our parents' actions, our parents' lives. We were not able to doubt and question what was happening to us. But most of all, we were not able to doubt or question God, for we feared instant destruction or even worse—we feared there would be no answer at all.

And yet, we had so many doubts and an infinite number of questions that could not be asked. We were afraid that our doubts would crumble what little safety and security there was in our lives. We were afraid our questions would draw people's anger and rejection. We were afraid our questions would only set us apart and keep us alone, letting everyone see our lack of belief.

It was not okay to doubt and question, for to do so would destroy the illusionary world we were living in, and we knew no other world. We were afraid our doubts would destroy what little love we experienced. We were afraid our questions would only answer our own fears that we were unworthy and unlovable.

And so, we hid all our doubts and all our questions, and in the darkness they grew and festered. They could not find release; they could not find the light, for it still was not okay to doubt and it still was not okay to question.

The gift of being able to doubt and question is truly a great freedom, a great release. This gift will show us that truth can always be doubted and always be questioned. For what is real will remain beyond all our doubts, and what is true will withstand all our questions. We bring our doubts to truth, so its light may dissolve each fear and answer fully each question.

The gift of being able to doubt and question is the gift of finding truth, for our Higher Power will invite all our doubts so that together we may discover His loving solution beyond each one. When we bring our doubts to truth, only what is true remains.

The gift of being able to doubt and question is our Higher Power's invitation to us to release all we hold and all we fear. It is an invitation to be and to express. It is an invitation of openness and honesty. Not only is it okay to doubt and question—it is the pathway to truth. And beyond all our doubts and questions are the gifts our Higher Power would give us to bring certainty to each doubt and truth to each question.

Bring your doubts to Me so I may reawaken the truth in you.

Bring all your questions to Me, for My love is the answer.

Bring your lack of faith, your lack of trust to Me, so I may give you what is honest and real.

Bring your uncertainties to me so I may give you My knowing.

Bring your fear that I will not answer, so I may show you, I am with you always.

THE GIFT OF BEING ABLE TO FEEL WHATEVER NEEDS TO BE FELT

It may not seem like a great gift... to be able to feel. We have spent much time and much effort in covering and suppressing our feelings. Much of our addictions have been to keep back feelings that continue to come relentlessly. We are afraid of feelings, for with most feelings, the intensity with which they come leaves us afraid and powerless. We think our strength comes from controlling our feelings and not allowing them to be seen and felt. We still believe that our safety is dependent upon keeping feelings in a place from which they cannot escape. We are afraid of being totally overwhelmed by our feelings. We fear this loss of control. So much of our efforts have gone into numbing, cutting off, and totally repressing our feelings, that we do not have any time or energy to live.

We have judged our feelings, condemned our feelings, and tried to erase our feelings. We have felt no support for our feelings, and cannot see any value in sharing them.

So effectively have we blocked off our feelings that we have also blocked off feelings of love, support, tenderness, gentleness, and happiness.

The gift of being able to feel whatever needs to be felt is a gift that will bring us back in touch with Life again. No longer will we have to hide and bury these feelings, but more importantly, no longer will we have to keep these feelings—feelings of despair, feelings of loneliness, feelings of hurt and judgment, feelings of shame and worthlessness, feelings of desperation, feelings of abandonment and terrible loss. Yes, we will feel these feelings again, but this gift is also their release. This gift is the safety with which healing can come. This is the gift that puts us in touch with pain that we have hidden, but it is also the gift that will release it and allow more room for happiness in our lives.

We can feel again. We can feel the care of each other. We can feel God's miracle of Life and Wonder. We can feel enthusiasm. We can feel laughter and we can feel the gift of tears. We can feel release and we can feel letting go of all that has hurt us. We can feel connected again with our Higher Power and His Love, and finally, we can feel what it is to BE—without judgment, without fear, without pain. We are in touch with ourselves again, and it is this that is our strength, our healing, and our reconnection with Life.

THE GIFT OF BEING ABLE TO PLAY

We have been taught that to learn anything, we must be serious. We have been taught that in order to accomplish anything, we must first be serious. We have been serious about life, we have been serious about our relationships, we have been serious about work and we have been serious about God and spirituality. Everything around us has been very serious.

The gift of being able to play, at first, seems a very frivolous gift, but it is the gift that lightens the heart and opens the door to let in all the joys and wonder of living. The gift of being able to play puts us in touch with that inner child who lives in beauty and innocence in all of us. The gift of being able to play embraces the moment; it lightens all burdens in its laughter at seeing: There is nothing so serious that our Higher Power cannot resolve in a loving way.

It is the gift in which we learn and know guidance. The gift of being able to play has no conditions. It is the essence of Joy; it is the center of Happiness. It is not a gift of acting or pretending, for that is what we have been so seriously trying to do. It is rather a gift of light-hearted freedom to be and express our truly joyous being.

It is a gift that allows laughter. It is a gift that includes everyone in our play. It is the gift that sees the child in everyone in all radiant innocence. With a light heart we see our Higher Power handling all our cares. With a light heart we are full of wonder at all the gifts coming into our lives. The gift of being able to play is the gift that says: "Unless we come as little children, we cannot enter into the kingdom of heaven."

The gift of being able to play is our entrance to the knowledge of heaven that is within us always.

THE GIFT OF BEING ABLE TO PRAY

Most of us have learned simple prayers as children. We memorized them and repeated them just as we were told. Later, in our childhood, we asked for God to answer certain desires and requests. And if He did not, in our opinion, answer these prayers to our liking, we grew doubtful and disappointed.

We saw those around us using prayer to try to get their way, to defend their cause—"God is on our side." We saw prayer being used to hide greed, control, and fanaticism. This prayer we did not want and could not understand. We began to see prayer as just one more manipulation.

Some of us still used prayer in a desperate attempt to have our difficulties solved. Our prayers were ones of avoidance—we sought to avoid rather than ask for healing. We hoped our prayers would be answered and what we thought would make us happy given to us.

Some of us have been unable to pray for a long time. Some of us have never been able to pray. Some of us are too embarrassed to pray—we do not wish to be like the "self-righteous" people we have seen using prayer. Some of us still wish to control our prayers and determine how they should be answered. Some of us simply don't know how to begin or what to say.

The gift of being able to pray is truly the gift of asking. We pray for the knowledge of God's Will for us. We pray for God's gifts to be given. We ask for God to be our prayer, because all the things we have prayed for have been to try to get what we thought would make us happy.

The gift of being able to pray is that gift of gentle asking that connects us with the love of our Higher Power. It connects us with the humility to ask for release from all we have made.

The gift of being able to pray is an admittance of what is truly in our hearts. It is an asking for what we have never been able to put into words. It is the knowledge that we, by ourselves, don't know, but with prayer we are immediately connected with all knowing.

The gift of being able to pray connects us with the Divinity within us. By the grace of prayer, we see where our true power lies. Prayer is not telling God what to do—it is asking God to come in. It is asking God to take what we have made and replace it with compassion and forgiveness.

We have demanded of God and we have used our prayers to try to get our way. But the Gift of Prayer is truly the gift of God's Way. Our prayers have only been for certain people, outcomes, and situations. The gift of prayer includes the healing of everyone. It includes everyone in its solution.

The gift of being able to pray allows us to give up what we have been trying to control in order to receive a loving solution.

The gift of being able to pray gives us the words we have never been able to find. It allows us to pour out our griefs, our resentments, our anguish, our fears. It allows us to go beyond these things to the purity of what we really want to say. The gift of being able to pray allows us to talk with our Source in all openness and honesty.

The gift of being able to pray opens the flow of our hearts. It opens our tears; it opens our Joy; it opens the way Home.

Prayer:

Give us this day Your daily Prayer.

Let this Prayer be one that would include everyone in its request.

Let Your Prayer bring peace to my heart.

Let Your Prayer bring forgiveness to my thoughts.

Let Your Prayer be my words.

Let Your Prayer be my truth and honesty.

Let Your Prayer be the way of a loving heart.

Let Your Prayer be my prayer.

--Amen

Speak to me of Your love.

Speak to me of Your care and wisdom.

Speak to me of Your gentle ways.

Speak to me of solutions beyond what the world has made.

Speak to me of love that I may give others.

Speak to me of Your gifts that I may receive and pass on.

Please be my speaking.

--Amen

THE GIFT OF BEING ABLE TO RECEIVE

We usually find it easier to give than to receive, simply because we feel more in control when we are giving. We have many fears about receiving—"Are there strings attached? Will I owe someone? How will I ever be able to repay it? What if someone is trying to manipulate me? What if I have to be responsible for whatever I receive?"

There are many fears about receiving. We even think we have to know how to receive, how to get out of the way, how to open up to receive the abundance of the universe. Many times we do not feel worthy of receiving gifts. We have judged ourselves as undeserving, and entitled to nothing. We have great difficulty receiving all that is ours. We fear receiving, we try to control receiving, and we reject receiving.

The gift of being able to receive is the gift our Higher Power gives us. By ourselves we have been unable to receive. Our Higher Power becomes the receiver. Our Higher Power is the Power with whom we are able to receive.

It is a gift our Higher Power keeps for us even if we have rejected all His gifts.

It is a gift that allows love into our lives. It is a gift that allows respect and caring to be ours. It is a gift that opens us to joy and happiness. It is a gift that brings us another way. And what we receive with this gift is truly God's wish of perfect Love, Peace, and Happiness for us. We receive God's Will and that Will is to be home with our Higher Power with all care, support, and well-being.

This gift is what we have to give. For if we are unable to receive, how then are we able to have anything to give? We receive the gift of receiving and in this are we given the gift of giving. For all we receive are we truly blessed, for this is our giving. We receive God's Gifts and we extend them. This is the gift of allowing all other gifts to be received in love, and given with our love. For this receiving are we truly grateful.

Dear Higher Power:

Will You receive for me today, all the gifts I have sought to keep away.

Will You receive for me today, all the support that is around me.

Will You receive for me today, what others are truly wishing to give me.

Will You receive for me today, the gift of Your Will.

Will You receive for me today, the gift of Receiving.

THE GIFT OF BEING IN THE MOMENT

Very seldom are we in the moment. We are either remembering the past or anticipating the future. We often miss the beauty of the moment. Seldom are we fully present where we are, aware of the perfection and the appropriateness of that very instant. We miss the very center which connects us with everything right at that moment. We are unaware of what surrounds us and of the gifts which are present.

The gift of being in the moment places us in full awareness of where we are now. It is the gateway to eternity and to what is eternally ours. In the moment do we receive each and every gift, for it is in the moment that any gift can be received. Being fully in the moment places us in the hands of our Higher Power. For that very moment are we guided and cared for. For that very moment are we surrounded in Peace and given direction. Being in the moment is the entrance to all solutions. When we are in the moment, it is impossible to judge, for all judgment is based either on the past or future. There is no regret in the moment. There is no fear in the moment.

We have thought that direction lay in anticipating the future, but true direction can only be given NOW. Everything unfolds from Now. When we anticipate the future, events do not unfold, they are manipulated. As absurd as it sounds, you cannot begin either in the past or the future, you can only begin NOW.

The gift of being in the moment allows us full appreciation of precisely where we are. It is a simple gratitude that we are in the appropriate place experiencing a deep connection with our Higher Power.

Being in the moment is the beginning of all prayer, for God can only be reached Now. God is Now and His Guidance extends through the Now into all eternity.

Being in the Now is that acceptance of truth, of joy, and of well-being beyond whatever seems to be happening. For that very moment we see our true nature and we see there will always be a solution—the solution of our Higher Power.

In the moment we are surrounded by the experience of Life.

In the moment we truly see another for the very first time.

In the moment we find guidance.

In the moment we see another way.

In the moment everything is seen clearly and in all of its perfection.

In the moment we find our connection with Oneness.

In the moment we are given all gifts.

And in the moment we are finally able to recognize the incredible value of these gifts and to know they are ours.

It takes but a moment and this moment is a gift our Higher Power gladly gives us. Can you take a moment? No, but it can be given. Can you find a moment? No, but it can be given. Can you understand a moment? No, but in a moment will all understanding come.

How do we live—moment by moment.

How do we see gratitude—in the moment.

What is our direction—to be in the unfoldment of the moment.

THE GIFT OF BEING OUTRAGEOUS

We have done many "outrageous" things from the depths of our desperation. We have performed many dangerous feats, trying to prove our bravery. We have walked close to the edge trying to overcome our fears. We have done spectacular and outrageous things trying to escape from a life of loneliness and despair. We have taken substances in order to come out of our self-imposed prison and we have performed "outrageously" towards those around us. People have not appreciated our outrageousness, for it came from a sense of fear. It came from wanting to prove we could be seen and heard. It came from being totally out of touch with our being.

If some of us acted outrageously, then others of us didn't come from out of our straightjackets at any time. We remained incased in our separateness and did not rock the boat or express ourselves at all. To be outrageous was not in our awareness for we were not aware of the beauty and depth of our being. To let our being be seen filled us with fear and apprehension. We preferred to hide.

The outrageousness we saw, was an act that came out of being separated from being, out of desperation, out of fear and pain. This outrageousness —the acting out of rage—brought much destruction and disconnected us even further from others and our Source.

The gift of being Outrageous is quite different from being out of rage. The gift of being Outrageous is a gift that truly shows us that it is okay to be. We have tried to conform or we have tried to rebel, but both of these have been from a sense of disconnection from our being.

The gift of Outrageousness says that it is okay to be. Truly, it is outrageous to be, because our doing is totally connected with our sense of being. We are at peace with our being and can express this with a wonderfully light heart. We can be outrageously happy because we are connected with the happiness of our being. We can be outrageously joyful, outrageously full of life. We no longer come from a rage; we come from the center of our being. We have stepped out of the rage that occurred when we could not see who we were, when we could not see Who walked beside us. We have stepped out of limits that have imprisoned us or limited the love, the gifts in our lives.

We can be outrageously in the moment. It is outrageous because we do not come seeking others' approval for what we do, yet we are full of consideration for others—we are outrageously connected with the Being of others.

Our being is outrageous because it has no limits or conditions. And in the limitlessness of our being are we fully aware and in tune with the beingness of others.

We no longer have to act out of rage because we no longer have to prove our being—it is a gift. Truly, outrageousness is the gift of being and expressing that being. We are not outrageous out of fear; we are outrageous out of the appropriateness of being.

With the gift of Outrageousness, we walk beyond our limits, our walls, our narrow thinking, our rigidity, into the light of being all we can be.

The gift of Outrageousness expresses the willingness to fully live and fully be with the fullness of our Higher Power's love. We are outrageously alive in His Being.

THE GIFT OF BEING REAL

The gift of being real is very simply the gift of being. We finally allow our being to express whatever it needs to express. The gift of being real does not mean our anger is real, our sadness is real, or our pain is real. It means we allow ourselves to feel and experience these things in order to come in touch with what is real. When we finally release all that has blocked our realness, we see the reality of a happy, joyous, and free being.

The process of recovery is truly recovering what is real—our innocence, our faith, our strength, our trust. In our recovery we allow what has covered this realness to be seen, heard, and let go. We recover our sanity. We recover our expression. We recover our strength and wisdom. We recover what is real.

The gift of being real is the gift of being able to look at what we have always sought to hide. It is the gift of being able to say:

> *"Everything that I have been using, hiding or avoiding is not really who I am."*

The gift of being real allows us to come from wherever we are without judgment. It allows us to begin without the fetters of guilt and condemnation. It allows us to admit our mistakes and ask for gentle correction. It allows us to be, so that we may be in touch with all that we are—so we may be in touch with our reality.

To be real is to be able to share where we are and what illusions we carry. In this sharing, the truth of who we are will be revealed.

The gift of being real is the gift of admittance. We admit or let in all our doubts, all our fears, and all our strange beliefs so that what is real may dissolve them and replace them with what is loving, what is true and what is healing.

The gift of being real is allowing our Higher Power to be our reality. It is the willingness to let our Source bring forth the reality in our lives.

Only what is wholly loving is true. And only what is wholly loving is real. All else, the gift of being real would take us beyond.

Our realness allows us to admit our anger. Our realness allows us to admit our resentment and thoughts of revenge. Our realness allows us to admit our doubts and lack of faith. Our realness allows us to admit when we are frightened and lost. Our realness allows us to feel whatever needs to be felt. Our realness allows all judgments and all our crazy thinking to be brought into the light.

The gift of being real encompasses all these things so that only what is real remains. We are willing to be all we can be—this is real. We are willing to have another way—this is real. We are willing to be of service—this is real. We are willing to let go, and we are willing to receive all the support our Higher Power has to give us—this is real. We are willing to accept ourselves in whatever way we are feeling and wherever we are coming from—this is real. We are willing to see the innocence of others beyond all illusions—this is real. We are willing to be guided, we are willing to be loving, we are willing to share what we have been and what we are now willing to be—this is real. We are willing to be in touch with our Source and from this, we are willing to be in touch with ourselves and others.

And what the gift of being real gives us is the knowledge that what is real has always been within us; has always been there for us to express and to be—this is reality.

We let the reality of our being shine away all illusions when we have the honesty to admit where we are, and what we are feeling.

The gift of being real is the power of honesty. We are honest enough to let people see those times when we are not being real, and in this honesty we are in touch with our realness.

Sometimes, people believe that in order to be real we must make everything real. No, illusions are still not real. The beliefs that cause pain and conflict are still not real. But in the freedom to admit everything, we allow what is real to shine away the darkness and in this we are in touch with our strength, our faith, and our reality.

We can allow everything through, because only what is real will remain. We admit the pain so that the realness of healing may give us a way of wholeness and release (real-ease).

Each gift is real, for only what is of God is real. His love is what heals. His truth is real. His understanding is real. His vision is the true vision. Being with God is the gift of being real.

THE GIFT OF BEING SEEN AND HEARD

We go to great lengths to be seen and heard by others. It is a deep desire within all of us. We have tried many ways to be seen and heard. We have used anger, being outrageous, rebellion, pleasing, accomplishments, shouting, appearances, reason, logic, leaving, and so on. Still, after all those things, we have never felt truly seen and heard. After all our efforts, manipulations, and desperation, after all our pushing and attempts to be seen and heard, we have not felt truly seen and heard at all. We have not felt seen for who we are, nor have we felt heard for what we have to offer.

The whole point is—we have not realized that being seen and heard is a gift. It is not something we have to struggle to achieve, for the very struggle keeps us from being either seen or heard. The very struggle keeps us from seeing and hearing others as well. The gift of being seen and heard places this responsibility in the hands of our Higher Power. With this gift He looks after both our being seen and our being heard.

The gift of being seen and heard does not have to prove anything, for we are seen for all our true value and we are heard for all the wisdom that is given to us. All our efforts to get people to see and hear us have hidden this gift from us. This is the gift of allowance—we allow our Higher Power to be what is seen and heard whenever we are present and whenever we speak.

The gift of being seen and heard will show others our innocence. It will show others our gifts and what we have to give. This gift takes care of being seen and heard for us. It sets us free from ever having to prove that we too have something to give.

Always before did we think we had to supervise being seen and heard. We supervised how people heard us; how people saw us; we supervised to make sure they followed through on what we tried to get them to see and hear. We were always supervising others in an attempt to be seen and heard. We called it by many names—we called it getting others to be considerate; we called it advice, education, "for your own good", sharing, caring for, worrying about, reason, logic, but behind all of these things was a desperation about being seen and heard. It was a pursuit that took much time and energy, but left us filled with resentment and despair at ever feeling seen and heard. We thought we could make people see and hear us, but we could not. We thought we could make ourselves seen and heard, but we could not. It is a gift that only our Higher Power can give and only when we accept this gift, the gift of our Higher Power's Vision and Hearing, will we be truly seen and heard.

THE GIFT OF BEING THERE FOR OTHERS

We often feel obligated to somehow be there for those in our lives. We feel obligated to know what to do, to know what to say, and to know how to fix any difficulties our loved ones are having. We feel obligated to listen and to console. We feel obligated to lend a helping hand. We feel obligated to be strong and to have a firm shoulder to lean on. We feel obligated to provide comfort, knowledge, and answers. We feel obligated to be there whenever we are needed.

It is a tall order to fulfill and most of us seem to fail in meeting all these prerequisites all the time. To make matters worse, when we are attempting to be there for one person, others in our lives feel resentful and neglected—why aren't we there for them? The more we try to oblige and be there for those people too, the more we end up pleasing no one. The more we try to be there for others, the less we are there for ourselves—the less nurturing we receive and the more tired and resentful we become.

It is an exhausting business trying to be there for others. And deep down there is a big doubt and a big fear—"I don't know how to be there for anyone. I can barely live my own life, what if I don't have any answers for others?"

The gift of being there for others is not a gift that places responsibility onto us. Being there for others is a gift—it is not a responsibility. We are not responsible for being there for others, but we are willing for our Higher Power to show us the most appropriate way to be respond-able. We are willing to be shown the most appropriate words to say, the most appropriate thing to do. With this gift, our own being comes in to play. It becomes a matter of being there with others. We share in our being and we allow others to be. We are given the gift of Listening. We are given the gift of Wisdom. We are given the gift of realizing that any "being there" has to include the nourishment of our being also.

The gift of being there for others is the recognition that we don't have all the answers; we don't know the best way to be there, but our Higher Power does. He will put us in touch with people at a moment when certain words are needed. He will put us in touch with the words. He will make sure we are available at the most appropriate time and place.

With this gift we will find ourselves calling at the most appropriate time, giving the most helpful answers and support. We will find ourselves doing what is most supportive with each person. With the gift of being there for others, we will see that it is truly being there, with our Higher Power giving the peace, giving the healing, giving the support and giving the love that is the true help and assistance for all those in our lives.

THE GIFT OF BEING TOTALLY AT PEACE WITH MYSELF

There seems to be a constant war within. Our mind seems to lecture at us continually. It tells us all the things we should be doing and are not. It tells us that what we are doing is inadequate and does not compare favorably with what others do. When we are doing one thing—we are told that we should be doing something else. When we are doing something else, we are told that we shouldn't be doing that, we should be doing still something else again. If we are working, then we should be spending more time with our family. If we are enjoying ourselves, then we should be more serious and dedicated to our accomplishments. If it is a nice day, we should be taking full advantage of it, and whatever we are doing isn't using the day to its full capacity.

We usually have several different voices telling us to do totally different things all at the same time. And all of these voices begin with: "You should!" and all of these voices end with, "Shame on you, you should feel guilty for all the things you are not doing right."

Within us we find ourselves criticizing what we say and how we say it. We find ourselves criticizing each and every decision we make by saying: "You should have chosen the other alternative." We find ourselves bringing in past decisions and choices to beat ourselves over the head with—"You should have done that, now look where you are."

We find ourselves bringing in past guilts in order to fuel present discomfort and pain. We find ourselves mulling over old anger and resentments. We become enmeshed in the "if only's". If only so-and-so loved me, if only I had said this or done that, if only I hadn't lost my job, my temper, my fortune, and so on, and so on.

Whatever choice we make has been the wrong one, and with this choice comes all the guilt and despair at having chosen wrongly once again.

Within ourselves we find a battle that cannot be won; we find a fight that never finds resolution and we find a circle that never sets us free.

The gift of being totally at peace with ourselves is the gift of having a tremendous burden literally taken away. It is the gift of being able to live with ourselves, not in constant torment, but in peace, in acceptance.

Imagine being able to hear the still, quiet voice within you, telling you that you are loved and accepted for whatever choice you make. Imagine a gift that shows you that whatever you do, you are still loved and appreciated.

Imagine being told that even if you make a mistake, that it is okay—it is all part of the process of learning to be. Imagine the gift of truly knowing that you are doing just fine, whether you made the best choice or not—you can always choose again. Imagine a gift where you could laugh at your seriousness, at your patterns, instead of condemning them.

The gift of being totally at peace with myself is a gift of friendship with myself. With this gift I am able to listen to my true desires and feelings. With this gift I am given respect for myself and for wherever I happen to be. With this gift I meet myself without judgment and am given an understanding to learn and to be whatever it is I need to experience.

With the gift of being totally at peace with myself, I may start from acceptance and open to being all I can be. With this gift there is no battle within, only support and encouragement to express, feel and share whatever is most appropriate for me in my well-being. This gift gives me back myself in all acceptance and all being. There is peace within and with this gift there is the friendship with myself within.

Instead of a million voices, all criticizing and giving different advice, I will find there is one voice, the Voice of my Higher Power speaking gently through me to say:

> *"My child can do no wrong. Go and do no wrong."*

THE GIFT OF BEING UNDERSTOOD

It is impossible to make sense out of insanity. Ultimately, it will be impossible to understand many insane behaviors simply because they are insane. Suffice it to say that when we are not in touch with what is in our hearts, when we are not in touch with the love, truth, and honesty within us, then we lose our center and our actions become insane. When we are not in touch with our Higher Power, we lose sight of Sanity.

We are not required to understand that which is insane, we are only asked to see that we have lost sight of Sanity. Often we wish desperately to be understood without realizing that much of the time we do not even understand our own thoughts, feelings, and actions. We feel misunderstood but do not know how to ask for understanding.

Truly, we have lost touch—we have lost touch with our Source and thus with ourselves. It is not the insanities in our lives that we wish understood; it is not the surface commotions for which we wish understanding. Truly, we each yearn to have the very heart and core of ourselves seen and understood.

We wish it to be understood that beyond all our crazy patterns there is clarity and wisdom. We wish others to understand that beyond all the selfish and controlling things that we have done and continue to do, there is someone truly wishing to be of love and service; someone wishing to do the best for everyone. We wish to be understood that beyond all our pettiness, resentments, and grievances there is someone who is loving and forgiving. We wish to be understood that beyond all our fears and weaknesses, there lays a heart of strength and courage.

We wish people to understand that behind our shyness, our awkwardness, is someone wanting to come out and play, wanting to come out and join with others in sharing. We wish people to understand that beneath all our mistakes and failures, there is someone wanting to do the very best, wanting to make the most appropriate choice. We wish people would understand that beyond all our controls, defects, and problems there is a someone who is centered and knowing. Beyond our sickness and seeming need for healing, there is a being who is complete and whole. We wish everyone to understand that beyond our struggles, conflicts and desperation, there is someone who simply wishes peace, who wishes another way. Beyond everything we wish to be understood for the child of innocence that we are.

Truly, we do not wish to be understood for the person we have made, for this is a protection and a defense—we wish to be understood for the being that we truly are beyond all pretending and pretense.

The gift of being understood takes us beyond our pretense and shows us that truly we are the very person we've always wanted to be.

The gift of being understood will allow us to understand ourselves. We will understand that it was only love and acceptance we sought in many crazy ways and forms. We will understand that all we wanted was to be loved and accepted for who we were.

The gift of being understood brings with it understanding. We will understand that we can ask for another way and be included in the solution. We will understand that we are forgiven and that we may forgive. We will understand that we are innocent and deserving of all gifts. We will understand that each moment we may let go of all our controls and insanities in order to be understood.

When I am willing to be honest, I am understood.

When I am willing to show where I am coming from, I will be understood.

When I am willing to let go, I will have the gift of being understood.

When I am willing to ask, I will be given understanding.

When I am willing to be guided, I will be understood.

When I ask for the gift of being understood, I will understand my own and others' innocence.

I understand that You are the Source through Whom I am understood and through Whom I find understanding.

The gift of being understood is truly having our hearts seen, having our hearts heard, having our hearts accepted, having our hearts loved.

With the gift of being understood, it is this understanding we will receive from our Higher Power:

I understand that you are seeing fearful things, but I see your light.

I understand you are feeling weak, but I see your strength.

I understand you are feeling resentful and angry, but I only see your innocence.

I understand you are feeling separate and alone, but I see your connection.

I understand you are feeling sick and afraid, but I see your completeness and wholeness.

I understand you are feeling lost and helpless, but I see that you are always with Me.

THE GIFT OF BEING WITH GOD

Oftentimes we have thought that we had to search to find God. We have looked for God in many strange places and by doing many strange things. We thought it was up to us to find God. We were uncertain on how to find Him, and once found, we were uncertain how to be with God.

The gift of being with God is a gift that lets us see God is always with us. We don't have to keep this awareness; it is a gift that will be constantly shown. God is always with us—this gift will show this reality to us in all circumstances and in everything that we do.

There is an old blessing—"God be with you." We will change it slightly to say: "May you always be aware that God is with you."

There is another blessing that says: "Go with God." This also we would rearrange to say: "God goes with you."

Really, what this gift brings is awareness. We have not seen God as always being with us and have thought it was up to us to know the way to God. This gift shows us that not only does God know the way —God is the Way.

The gift of being with God is the gift of knowing we are always with God. It is a gift of certainty.

The gift of being with God is really the only gift there is, for that is the gift we treasure most of all. And in that Gift are all other gifts found.

Our being is with God. The gift of being with God is truly being able to express our being.

THE GIFT OF BLESSINGS

To bless is to release. Truly, in counting our blessings we are seeing what we have released to God. What we bless is released. Many times it has been said: "Bless them and release them."

To bestow a blessing on someone is truly to let them go. We bless them so that they, too, may claim the healing gifts that God holds for them.

To bless is to recognize the gifts that are ours. It is the recognition that what we give to others, we keep as our own blessing.

To bless is to let in light. We ask God to shine upon our brothers. When we see how we are blessed, we see the light that surrounds us.

To bless is to forgive. In blessing, we can hold no resentments, no anger, no darkness. We bless because in doing so, this gift we receive also.

To bless is to recognize the gift another has given us. With this recognition, we feel the source within us and say—"God bless you."

"Blessed child of God, help us see our true worth and our true inheritance."

To bless another is to see him for who he truly is. The gift of blessings is the gift of passing on God's gifts to all we meet. We are blessed, and with this blessing do we have the gift of extending blessings.

We are blessed because we may ask for all gifts. We are blessed because in sharing these gifts our blessings multiply one-thousand-fold.

Blessed are those who ask for another way, for they will go beyond all pain and despair.

Blessed are those who ask for help from a Higher Power, for they will see the power within.

Blessed are those who ask, for they shall be answered.

Blessed are those who pray, for they shall receive guidance.

Blessed are those who forgive, for they shall see innocence.

Blessed are those who ask for faith, for they shall be given direction.

Blessed are those who ask for knowing, for they will be given compassion.

Blessed are those who ask for strength, for they shall be given gentleness.

Blessed are those who give the gift of blessings, for they shall be blessed with each gift our Higher Power has to give.

Blessed are those who ask to be with God, for they shall never be alone and without blessings.

In God are we blessed.

In God do we bless.

In God is our blessing.

THE GIFT OF CELEBRATION

Most of our "celebration" has been an attempt to escape from our pain. Our celebrations have been an effort to close areas where we have felt helpless and ineffectual. We have celebrated a difficult task that we have finally accomplished. We have celebrated events. But quite often we use these occasions as another excuse to escape our fears and desperations.

The gift of Celebration is not something we use to escape—it is a gift that invites Life in. We celebrate the life around us. We celebrate the life within us. We celebrate each opening that another is willing to make. We celebrate what we truly have to offer. We celebrate the gift of support that is always there for the asking. We celebrate the joy that is behind each feeling that we feel. We celebrate the solutions that come when we ask for another way.

We celebrate being in touch with all that we are. We celebrate healing. We celebrate the wisdom that is in each one of us. We celebrate our ability to be. We celebrate the beauty of each moment. We celebrate with laughter that connects us with the essence of gratitude. We celebrate our full capacity to express all our caring, all our knowing, and all our love. We celebrate all judgments dropping away. We celebrate the innocence that we see as each child of God steps forth from his place of hiding. We celebrate a faith that is given. We celebrate a new way of thinking, feeling and being. We celebrate recovery from all pain and illusion. We celebrate the simplicity of truth, the simplicity of asking, the simplicity of answers, the simplicity of life, the simplicity of joy.

We celebrate beginning again—having all mistakes forgiven. We celebrate the freedom that comes when we let our Higher Power heal each situation.

To celebrate is to express ourselves to the fullest, letting all our joy and wonder of life flow from us. To celebrate is to join with others in the fullness and acceptance of our beings. We celebrate Life together. We celebrate with gratitude, for gratitude is the heart of the gift of Celebration.

To celebrate is to invite Life in, and with this invitation we invite others to join the celebration.

Let us celebrate living,

Let us celebrate beginning,

Let us celebrate the doing,

Let us celebrate completion,

Let us celebrate each other,

Let us celebrate our being,

Let us celebrate the breath of Life,

Let us join together and celebrate
our oneness,

Let us celebrate the God within,

Let us invite God to be our celebration.

THE GIFT OF CERTAINTY

Certainty is not the absence of doubts. We do not receive this gift by keeping doubts away or denying them. Certainty is a gift that can take any doubt and shine its light of truth upon it. It is, then, the certainty that any doubt, problem, illusion, or fear can be gone beyond.

The gift of Certainty acknowledges all doubts, and in doing so allows what is true, what is real, to be seen. It is a knowing which says: any doubt, any illusion, any problem, any impossibility can be seen through and another way can be given.

Certainty allows all things simply because it can withstand all illusion. It can withstand any questioning or inspection. It can even withstand our attempts to change it, for the truth cannot be changed and this is certain.

The gift of Certainty is a deep knowing that takes us beyond all appearances. It is a certainty that if anything is causing us pain, there is another way of seeing that will be given to us, there is another solution that will bring us healing.

The gift of Certainty brings with it a deep sense of peace that our asking will always be answered. It brings a certainty that the answers we receive will always be from love and always be for our well-being.

If we are choosing our solutions, we will be very uncertain indeed. We cannot ask for certainty in our solutions because our solutions have always been the problem.

The gift of Certainty tells us that God always has a solution, and that we can be certain that His Solution is always the most appropriate one; always the most healing one.

When we are uncertain, we may ask for the certainty of God's solutions instead of our own.

The greatest connector with certainty is gratitude. The moment we are grateful for anything—certainty appears. Gratitude and certainty go heart in heart. With certainty that our Higher Power is the solution, we can be grateful. In gratitude for all we are given, we are certain that all gifts, all answers are ours. Certainty is the heart of knowing, and gratitude is the heart of certainty. In this gift are we connected to all things, for certainty must include the true awareness of everything.

We don't have to be certain about people, places, or things, but we are asked to be certain that whatever we turn over to our Higher Power can be used for healing.

If we are uncertain about which direction to take, about which goal to choose, about how to live our lives, about the next step, then we have simply lost our focus. For certainty does not come from the direction we go or from the steps we choose; it comes from a simple asking to be with God. Certainty is the Spirit of God working, living, and breathing through all things. Certainty is another name for God and in choosing to put God first in our lives, we instantly receive this wonderous gift. God is at the heart of all certainty and with a little gratitude we are connected with the certainty of our Source.

I am certain that if I ask, You will be with me.

I am certain that any problem I give to You will have a loving solution.

I am certain that You are my knowing.

I am certain that Your Love will heal whatever has brought me pain.

I am certain that there is always a way of peace that You will show me.

I am certain that beyond my doubts You will show me Your Truth.

I am certain that when I have no willingness, You will give me Your strength.

I am certain that when I am afraid, You will bring Your Light to comfort me.

I am certain that when I am lost, You will guide me.

I am certain that when I lack certainty, You will give me Your Faith.

I am certain that Your gifts will lead me Home.

THE GIFT OF CHOICE

We have desperately tried to control many events and people in our lives because we did not see there was a choice. We carried much anger and rage because we did not see there was a choice. We were sad, bitter, and resentful. We did not see we had a choice.

Now we begin to hear about acceptance and forgiveness and we are fearful because we do not see the gift of Choice. Our choices have been choices of suspicion and distrust. We have chosen to go it alone and we have chosen our separate ways. Our choices have been ones of reaction and revenge. Our choices have seemed to be ineffectual and to lead nowhere. Our choices were borne out of control and perpetuated the fear in which they were made.

Now we are told to let in a Higher Power. This seems to leave us without choice at a time when we feel more frustrated than ever.

What choice do we have?

The gift of Choice is given us by our Higher Power. This gift will help us choose another way. This gift will always help us choose what is most appropriate for our lives to be completely healed. The gift of Choice will direct us to allow what is loving, supportive, and joyous into our lives.

Our choice is directed now—it is directed by One Who only has our well-being at heart.

The gift of choice is essential for our healing, for without it we will continue to feel controlled and, consequently, we will feel we must continue to control.

With this gift, we ask you to consider: What if you could let everything in without resistance and still have the choice to do what was appropriate for you? What if you could let in all ideas and suggestions, and still have a choice to be and express Who you truly are? What if you could accept each situation and each person and still have a choice to be guided in what was most loving for you?

You see, the Gift of Choice, given to us by our Higher Power, always allows us to choose what is best for us in terms of happiness, health, love, expression, growth, support and all other gifts that bring us in touch with our own true nature and bring us in touch with the guidance of our Higher Power.

It is essential to see this gift of Choice. We have a choice now that is given to us each moment. It is a choice for peace instead of conflict. It is a choice for happiness instead of misery. It is a choice for healthy expression instead of condemnation. It is a choice for Being instead of judgment. It is a choice for Life instead of death.

> *"Give us this day our daily choice... give us Your Choice here."*

We have tried to control situations where we did not see we had a choice. We may speak about acceptance, forgiveness, allowing, and letting go. We may speak of letting in and consideration, but until we see we have a choice and that choice is always for our well-being, we will not understand or trust the whole process of letting go and letting God.

The only choice we really have is when we give up our choice and ask God to be our choosing.

When we ask God to be our choosing, we realize that God is our choice.

Invariably, if we make a choice from a desire to control, we may be assured that ultimately that choice will not be in our best interest. If we allow or ask our Higher Power for the gift of Choice, that choice will be for everyone's healing and happiness.

THE GIFT OF COMPLETION

We have thought that to be complete with someone was an ending. If you complete a job, that seems to be the end of it with no change possible. If you complete a relationship, that also seems to be the end of the relationship. Quite often we don't like to complete things because we see them as an ending. We have left many things uncompleted because we feared things coming to an end where there was sadness or pain remaining.

But the gift of Completion sees things differently. When we are complete with someone, we have finally let go of any resentments, any misperceptions, any blocks to love with that person. We have let go and allowed that person to be. We need not fix this person, change this person, nor control this person. We simply allow them to be. We are complete with them. This is not an end. This completion allows us to be with this person in total love, support, and caring whether we stay with them or choose to be in another place. This completion allows us to begin living in joy, in freedom, and in genuine caring.

With the gift of Completion in our lives, we are complete with each situation or circumstance when we finally let go of any resentments, desperations, expectations, projections, and attachments connected with that situation. In other words, our peace is no longer dependent on the circumstance, but may be expressed through the situation. We are complete with the situation—not so it can come to an end, but so we may begin to allow life's unfoldment to work through us in whatever we choose to do and with whomever we choose to be with.

In one sense, completion will be an end—the end of any pain, misery and resentment we have held with a person or situation. Just like we are not afraid of Love, but of the controls that Love would dissolve, likewise we are afraid of all the controls that will be lost when completion occurs.

Truly, incompletion is being without God. Incompletion is thinking that we have to do it alone.

The gift of Completion is truly the gift of letting go in order to allow the flow of life to enter and guide us. We are complete knowing that God guides us in whatever we do. Therefore, we may allow many things to be completed in order to let them go, to let them be, and to let them unfold. We complete through forgiveness, through acceptance, and this becomes our doing.

The gift of Completion is the gift of letting go. We complete things not as an end, but as a beginning to letting in more life, more direction, more loving, and the unfoldment of God's eternal healing.

THE GIFT OF CONSIDERATION

The gift of consideration is simply the gift of open-mindedness. It is the gift of allowing something in, in order to see another way. So often we are afraid to consider anything because we feel obliged to do whatever is considered. We feel that if we consider something, we have to do it. If we consider a suggestion, we feel we have to follow it. If we consider an idea, we feel we have to believe it. We do not see that we have a choice.

The gift of consideration helps us to allow in everything so we may see our choice of always doing what is most appropriate for our own and others' well-being. To be considerate does not mean to do, it only means to allow in, in order to see the best possibilities and solutions.

We consider that there may be another way. We consider the possibility of another way of seeing. With the gift of consideration, a tiny gateway is opened for all solutions to be given.

When we consider what another says to us—we are considerate. When we consider, we may be guided to say "yes" or "no". To consider, then, is to let in. And what we let in is the guidance for all solutions.

The gift of consideration shows us the choice we always have when we allow our Higher Power to run our lives.

We are not asked to know what the solutions are to our difficulties—we are only asked to consider that our Higher Power may be the solution in each difficulty.

Consideration opens our mind to all the possibilities. Consideration takes us beyond judgment. Consideration is a focus on solutions.

Consideration lets in others so we may see the gifts they may have to give. Consideration and choice go hand in hand.

To be considerate of another is the gift of allowing that person in. We still have the choice to do and to be what is best for us.

The gift of consideration is what takes us beyond all that we fear and resist. A tiny willingness to consider is the turning point where another way of healing may enter.

THE GIFT OF CREATIVITY

Creativity is a life-flow that has its source in our Higher Power. To create anything, then, is to reconnect with our Source. What we create is a form that expresses the Source and in expressing the Source, ultimately goes beyond form to spirit. True creativity is extending the love, the understanding, the caring of our Higher Power. Creativity is the spirit of truth expressing its essence through us and all that we do.

The gift of Creativity is a gift that begins without judgment. When there is no judgment, the flow of creativity is unhampered by any restrictions. When there are no judgments, the flow of creativity is full and immediate.

With the gift of Creativity, we open to express all that we are. The gift of Creativity allows us to share the Source with others—to give it expression. There is an endless number of ways to connect and express the God within—this limitlessness is creativity.

Truly, the freedom to express wherever we are coming from gives us a connection to creativity. Creativity, then, is being able to express whatever comes from our hearts, whatever needs to be said, whatever needs to be asked.

The gift of Creativity puts us in touch.

We are in touch with our boundless expression.

We are in touch with joy.

We are in touch with what has brought us sadness.

We are in touch with pain.

We are in touch with our deepest desires.

We are in touch with our gifts.

We are in touch with our fears.

We are in touch with our innocence.

We are in touch with ourselves.

We are in touch with our being.

The gift of Creativity is truly the unbounded expression of our being. It is the expression of our connection with Life. It is the expression of our connection with God.

The gift of Creativity allows us to be who we are and with this being, to connect with others through creative expression. An opportunity is created where forgiveness and healing may occur. An opportunity is created where we may extend love rather than resentment.

The gift of Creativity is a gift that is shared. We share our being and we share our most holy relationship to the God within.

The gift of Creativity is truly to let Life flow through us—life in all its expressions, and ultimately in all its Truth.

The gift of Creativity is our expression of honesty. We express honestly what we feel, what we see, where we are. But the gift of Creativity takes us beyond all these things to set free the eternal moment. It is creative because it is Now. It is creative because it sets free the moment.

It is said that someone who is creative captures the moment—but we say—the gift of Creativity releases and sets it free.

The gift of Creativity is truly God talking through us. It is our connection. We are part of God—we are part of everything.

The gift of Creativity expresses our oneness using unlimited form. With the gift of Creativity, we are all that we can be in joyful expression and from this being, we give the gift of Creativity for all others to join in this expression.

Question: Is pain necessary to be more creative?

Answer: No.

Truly, creativity is an expression. We do not deny our pain—we express it. Creativity really has nothing to do with pain—it has everything to do with being in touch with what needs to be said or expressed. Creativity may express pain, but the true gift of Creativity will always release and take us beyond. It is like seeing Christ on the cross. If we focus on pain, we forget the message is resurrection; we forget the message is—Life Eternal beyond our worst fears of death.

Creativity will always show us the Life, the Joy, present in every situation. It will not deny what is happening, but it will show us a gateway to the Light, to another way.

Creativity might not always express joy. It may express what brings us doubt and confusion. But in that expression there will be the possibility of release. There will be the possibility of going beyond wherever we find ourselves to the joy of Life; there will be an asking to be reconnected with our Source.

Returning to the Source is creativity (Re-Source-Fullness). Bringing out all doubts that block the Source is creativity. Expressing where we are coming from is the gift of Creativity. Allowing ourselves to be is creativity. Creativity always expands our being and puts us in touch with all that we are. All of God's gifts express creativity. Allowing the flow is creativity, for creativity is the flow.

Ultimately, the only true creation is the Love of God, the Peace of God, the Joy of God. To see God is our being gives us the unlimited gift of Creativity.

THE GIFT OF EASE IN EVERYTHING THAT I DO

When we are into management, we tend to complicate things endlessly. There is much effort and difficulty in trying to obtain our goals and pursue what we think would make us happy. We are use to struggle and pain as we go through life. There is a saying which says: *"Nobody said it was going to be easy."*

The gift of Ease is being with our Higher Power. With this gift, direction and solutions unfold naturally and easily. The gift of Ease occurs when we finally let our Higher Power manage our lives. "Easy does it," is very simply: Letting God or Ease do it. God is Love and God is Ease. Just as Love is expressed by being with our Higher Power, so is Ease expressed in all that we do by letting our Higher Power be the Ease with which it is done.

The gift of Ease allows us to go with the flow without having to insist on our usual struggle to swim upstream. There is an ease in feeling and there is an ease in simply being. There is an ease in the love that comes into our lives and there is an ease in sharing with others. Being with God, all is done with Ease, because it is Ease or God that does it.

We have believed that struggle is imminent or essential to accomplish anything, for our true struggle has been trying to live a life based on our own will, apart from God. The only struggle there really is, is trying to live without the direction and guidance of our Higher Power—we have been Power-less. Our difficulties have arisen from our struggles to live a life based on self-will and beset with goals that we thought would make us happy. The conflict is believing that there is still an area that we can manage better than our Higher Power. Struggle is ego-centered. Ease is God-Centered. With God in our lives...

"Nobody said it was going to be difficult."

THE GIFT OF ENTHUSIASM

Our lives have been full of have-to's. Each day we have had a list of things we have to do. As the day is never long enough to do all the have-to's, we soon have a backlog of things we have to do. Our pile of have-to's gets bigger and bigger and more urgent with each passing day. The more we have had to do something, the more we have been resistant to doing it.

We have not liked have-to's, but we have not really seen that we are the ones who make ourselves have to do anything. We have to keep our appointments. We have to be nice. We have to be a certain weight. We have to look good. We have to work hard. We have to do our work well. We have to earn good money. We have to be successful.

We have to be married. We have to be in a relationship. We have to be loved. We have to be there for people. Our children have to obey us. We have to say, do and eat the right things. We have to get our sleep. We have to have time for ourselves. We have to meet our commitments. We have to go places.

We have to supervise others to make sure they are doing things right. We have to shape up others. We have to fix and change those around us. We have to save the world.

We have to be on time. We have to keep up with things. We have to be busy. We have to have more fun in our lives. We have to listen to people. We have to help people. We have to learn things. We have to be smart. We have to have something to say. We have to be creative and amusing. We have to be strong. We have to have it together. We have to do our duty. We have to meet family obligations. We have to phone people, write people, visit people. We have to keep in touch with people. We have to know what's going on. We have to have a clean home. We have to perform. We have to get up in the morning. We have to be spiritual and enlightened. We have to accomplish things. Everything becomes a have-to.

It is difficult to imagine a life without have-to's—"But I have to have have-to's, how will I get anything done?" Actually when we have to do something, we immediately resist doing it at all. We resent have-to's and do them most grudgingly.

The gift of Enthusiasm takes us beyond have-to's and shows us the gift of choose-to's. Have-to's do not give us a choice. The gift of Enthusiasm shows us the choice of doing those things, which are for our well-being and for others' well-being. The gift of Enthusiasm is the gift of doing out of a healthy, joyous choice. We choose to do from the spirit of Enthusiasm. We choose to do from the spirit of light-heartedness and joy. We are enthusiastic for life and our choices reflect this.

The gift of Enthusiasm is truly the gift of being in God—Entheos.

The gift of Enthusiasm shows there is always a choice to do what is most loving for everyone. It is the gift of whole-heartedness. When we have to do something, we express ourselves half-heartedly. With the gift of Enthusiasm, we can whole-heartedly be present to express the joy of our being through whatever we do.

The gift of Enthusiasm is a zest for Life and the expressing of that Life. It is a gift of living Life to the fullest with all our hearts.

We don't have to accept this gift. This may be done for us also. We don't have to do anything, but with the gift of Enthusiasm, what cannot be done for healing, for joy, for being, for expression, for creativity?

We don't have to be with God. No one is making us. It is a gift. No one is making us live—it is a gift. No one is making us do—it is a gift of choice. No one is making us be—it is a gift. Nothing is made—all is given. The gift of Enthusiasm is the gift of doing everything with the spirit of God. This is the gift with which we express our Being. This is the gift with which we may chose to express the presence of God in all that we do.

THE GIFT OF EXPRESSION

There is a lot of judgment on our expression. Our expression is very limited. We have judged that it is not okay to express certain fears, doubts, questions, desires, feelings, emotions, and even happiness. Some of us have judged everything we express and consequently can express nothing without fear of condemnation.

We have not known how to express certain things, for we did not feel gifted to express anything. For some things we simply did not have the words. For other things we were so cut off from the things we wanted to express that we had only a vague idea of what the expression was.

Some of us had never felt safe to express. It was not safe to express our fears, our anger, our creativity—it was not safe to express our Being.

We are very rusty at expressing anything from our hearts. We have expressed confusion, commotion, depression, repression, niceness, feeling "fine", and feeling numb. But deep within we know that this is not what we wish to express at all, for it does not come from our hearts—it comes from a fear to express.

We wish to give you the gift of Expression. In reality the only true expression is when we give all our expression to our Higher Power for His gift of Expression.

With the gift of Expression we become able to express whatever is needed without having to judge it. With this gift we will be able to express in the most appropriate surroundings and with the most appropriate people all that we have feared to express.

We have forgotten how to express joy—this gift will teach us.

We have dreaded to express sadness—this gift will give us the courage to release those feelings and memories that we have been unable to share.

We have forgotten how to express our creativity—this gift will bring us in touch with all we have to give and express in many wonderous forms.

We have judged the ability to express love, fearing it would make us vulnerable and open to hurt once more. This gift will show us the well-spring of Love that is constantly flowing within us. This gift will BE the expression of all the Love we wish to feel and to give.

Behind all our expressions of hatred, fear, and pain is the expression of the joyous being within us.

We will be given the expression of our inner child, of the child-like innocence that we have always wished to express.

With the gift of Expression, our Higher Power will lovingly encourage that expression, nurture that expression, guide that expression, and maintain that expression. For ultimately, our Higher Power becomes the Expression in our lives.

We have forgotten that expression does not always need words. With the gift of Expression, we will be shown countless ways of expressing who we are. We will receive the gift of expression in all areas of our lives and this expression will heal all those that it touches, for this expression comes from Truth.

We will be able to express our Higher Power's love through tears, through laughter, through smiles, through being present, through our acceptance, through touching and being touched, through silence, through simply being. Whatever is appropriate will be expressed in the most appropriate way.

The gift of Expression is what allows us to share where we are coming from, what we have resisted, what we have feared, what we have truly desired, and the answers we have been given.

With this gift, God becomes the Expression with which we live and share. With this gift we express Life and the Joy within it.

Dear Higher Power:

Would You be my expression today.

Would You help me to express any sadness I need to feel.

Would You help me to express any doubts I have been hiding.

Would You help me to express any dishonesty, so I may come clean.

Would You help me to express any hatred I hold, so I may be given forgiveness.

Would You help me to express any tears that I have been holding.

Would You help me to express my fears, so I may see they are nothing when Your Light is shone upon them.

Would You be my expression of creativity, so I may express Your Love in whatever I do.

Would You express my desire to connect and share with others.

Would You be my expression of Love, so I may show others the deep love I feel for them.

Would You be my expression of Joy, for I've never truly known how to express the joy of Life.

Would You be my expression of prayer to ask You for guidance, to ask You for healing.

Would You be the expression with which I receive all Your Expression.

--Amen

THE GIFT OF FAITH

We have difficulty in admitting that we do not know. We still believe, at times, that our management will provide the answer. We have difficulty in admitting that we don't know today, and we won't know tomorrow either. We have a great resistance to letting people see we don't know. We don't know how to love, how to be "there" for others, how to produce, how to find our worth, how to find safety, how to be in the now, how to do the appropriate thing, how to provide for others, how to find the right direction.

Some of us even use, "I don't know how," so that knowing will never be required of us. Some of us use, "I don't know, but I want to impress you that I'll have it together tomorrow."

Finally admitting that we don't know is not to use it; it is rather the admittance that lets in our Higher Power.

This is when the gift of Faith is possible. The gift of Faith allows us to admit we do not know—but faith steps in and says we will be given knowing.

The gift of Faith allows us to admit that we do not know which way to go, but we will be given direction. The gift of Faith puts us in touch with our not knowing so we may see that all knowing, all guidance comes from our Higher Power.

The gift of Faith helps us to admit that even if we don't know how to be there for others, we will be guided with all appropriateness and with all caring.

The gift of Faith lets us admit without judgment that we don't know and that is okay, because our knowing has never brought us peace. We wish the knowing of our Higher Power.

The gift of Faith is the Faith of our Higher Power. We do not have to make it up. We do not have to know where to find it—it is a gift.

We are given Faith to see that whatever is turned over to our Higher Power will be healed in the most appropriate way. We are given Faith to see the limitless strength of love that will be given when we feel no love or have no love to give.

The gift of Faith is the knowledge that whatever we lack in our awareness will be given when we admit that by ourselves we don't know, we don't have enough—we are empty.

Prayer:

Please fill me with Your Faith where I see myself as lacking.

Please help me to admit I do not know, so I may be given Your Knowing.

Please help me see with Your Faith all the innocence that surrounds me.

Please give me the Faith to see I will be given Your gifts always.

Please give me the Faith to place my faith in You.

--Amen

THE GIFT OF FEELING AT HOME

Always have we looked to the outside to provide us with the feeling of being at home. Some places seemed to give us a sense of home, but mostly we felt at home nowhere. Our constant search had been a search for home, for a sense of belonging and connection. With a sense of despair we had not found that home, nor had we found what might give it to us.

The gift of being at home is a gift that comes from within. We are finally at home with our Higher Power, and with this gift we are at home with ourselves. The gift we have always wanted is within us. Our search for home has been a search for our Higher Power. We are at home only in Him. The home we seek is not to be found outside of ourselves. When we feel at home with our Higher Power and His Will, we will feel at home everywhere. He is our sanctuary. He is our safe-keeping. He is where we will feel at Home.

THE GIFT OF FEELING AT ONE

When we are at one, we are at the center of all things. We feel connected; we feel at peace. The gift of feeling at one connects us with all Life. We feel a kinship with our fellow travelers and realize we are not on this journey alone. We are in touch with the naturalness of each thing we do and each thing that happens. We see life unfolding in a most miraculous way. We are full of a sense of wonder. With the gift of being at one, we no longer focus on differences—we focus on the part each one of us plays in completing the whole.

With the gift of Oneness, we are in touch with our completeness and we are able to see others in their completeness.

The gift of feeling at one is not having to be the same as everyone else; it is the gift of being able to express our entire capacity of creativity in order to add to the wholeness of everything.

The gift of feeling at one is the recognition we are at home wherever we happen to be. We recognize love and are at one with it—we recognize that is Who we are. We recognize joy and realize joy is us. We recognize brotherhood and realize we are our brother. We recognize truth and see the truth within us.

Each one of us can express God in many loving ways—these ways are the Oneness.

With the gift of Oneness, we do not lose our individuality, for truly our individuality has been very limiting. With the gift of feeling at one, we see we are everything and Who we are knows no bounds.

The gift of feeling at one brings us home to our Higher Power, for truly we can only be at one with God. We are at one with His

Peace, His Joy, and we are at one with each other. In this there is no limitation.

I am at one with you in all our differences.

I am at one with you in the love we are.

I am at one with you in the God that is within us.

I am at one with you in both our healing and our release.

I am at one with you in all the gifts we have to give and to share.

I am at one with you in our innocence.

I am at one with you in being at home with our Higher Power.

I am at one with Life—I am at one with Joy.

I am at one with all living things.

I am at one with You.

THE GIFT OF FEELING TOTALLY ALIVE

So often we think we must pursue life, and anytime we find it, we believe we must grasp or hold on to it with all our strength. We feel we must look for life and we feel we must maintain any life that we find. Often we confuse life with the adrenaline rush of excitement. There are certain things or addictions that we believe "make" us feel alive, and we are not happy, we are not "alive", without these experiences.

The fact that life is a gift still eludes us. So long have we pursued what we thought would make us feel alive that we have not seen this simple truth—Life is a gift. If we pursue life, we will not see it is ours already. Life will be forever something we are chasing, never to quite catch up to it. If we grasp life, we also lose sight that it is a gift, for our grasping will only choke off our feeling alive, and leave us fearing the loss of this aliveness.

The gift of feeling totally alive is not dependent on any person, place or experience. Because it is dependent on nothing outside of us, the aliveness is total. There are no external conditions or limitations. The gift of feeling totally alive is ours right now—we do not have to pursue it; we do not have to grasp or hold on to it. It is not dependent on our experience or any addiction. In other words, the whole preciousness of this gift is that we can be given this gift without any of these conditions or desperations.

The gift of feeling totally alive is maintained for us. It is the great gift of being able to feel, and what we feel is the gift of aliveness beyond all feelings. We can finally feel and release all we feel. We can feel fully—and all that is not Life is released.

The choice for Life is the choice to feel. The choice to feel is to finally be in touch with that gift of Life, with that gift of aliveness that dissolves all sorrows, all blocks, and all limitations.

The gift of feeling totally alive can be likened to taking in a full breath and, just as fully, releasing it. We are in touch with all our being. We are in touch with all loving expression. We are in touch with those around us. We are in touch with a tremendous joy of living—NOW. But most of all, we are in touch with the Spirit of God, alive and well within us.

Like any other gift, to keep it, we let it go by sharing it. In remembrance we give our gifts away only to see them increased one-hundred-fold. We open to Life by a willingness to share Life. We find Life in our Higher Power. We find Life in sharing our aliveness with others. We are even given the gift of opening to Life so it may fill us with all its caring, all its compassion, all its vitality, and all its enthusiasm. The gift of Life, the gift of feeling totally alive, is simply our willingness to let our Higher Power express through us at all times.

Prayer:

You are the Life with which I breathe.

You are the Life with which I live.

You are the Life with which I love.

Your Life is my being—You are my GIFT.

You are the Life within me, flowing to encompass all things with its Love.

--Amen

THE GIFT OF FINDING THE GIFT IN EVERYONE

There are many people in our lives that we sometimes wish were in someone else's life instead. Why do they have to be in our life? Even those that we tolerate in our lives often seem to need vast improvement. And those near and dear to us often lose their preciousness when we focus on all the things they could and should be doing.

We see how we could fix people, how we could change them for the better. We see how they could be helped, how their lives could be organized, how their lives could be rearranged. We know the advice we would give them that would work wonders for their improvement. We have the answer for those that plague us—we would like to be rid of them and to tell them to get lost. We would tell them a very interesting thing—we would tell them to "Get out of my face." We have the answer to those that annoy us—"Don't bug me. Leave me alone." We have the answer for those close to us—"Let me guide and direct you. You could do so much better with my help."

However, with all our wanting to be rid of, with all our good intentions, helpful hints, improvement plans, and down right interference, we miss something very important—we miss seeing the gift in each person. We miss seeing the beauty of a being emerging in their own grace, in their own light and in their own wisdom and knowing. We miss seeing the opening of a beautiful flower, glowing in its own radiance.

When we allow someone to be, we are given a tremendous gift—we start to truly see them. We start to see their beauty and their wisdom. We start to see their innocence—fragile at first, but growing stronger and stronger in the joy of awareness and recognition. We start to see a being in touch with its own healing powers, with its own God connection. We start to hear and see the gift that each person has to offer.

With the gift of seeing the gift in everyone, we put aside our judgments; we put aside our doubts; we put aside our prejudices and our improvement plans and we are given the gift of not only truly seeing someone, but we are given the gift of what they have to offer.

The gift, when we see it, is a very surprising one—for it is the gift of ourselves. The gift that each person has to offer is the gift of seeing ourselves. Each person will give part of ourselves back into our awareness.

Each person we meet has the gift for us to see our own innocence, our own courage, our own child.

The gift of seeing the gift in everyone is truly the gift of:

> *"There by the grace of God go I. By the grace of God I see myself in each one I meet. I see myself with all my fears, with all my hurts, and with all my pain. But, I see myself with all my willingness and my true desire to be well and joyful again. I see in each one I meet, the gift of never having to be alone again. I see my journey reflected in the eyes of these gifts. And I see my journey's end and my Life's beginning in each gift I allow to be and to show me what God would offer me through them."*

The gift of seeing the gift in everyone is the gift of meeting ourselves and the beauty of this gift is that this encounter is always a holy one.

I see you in me.
When I let you be.
To be all that you are.
This sets us free.

I see you in me.
And what I find.
Is that we are One.
In spirit and in mind.

Prayer:

Please show me the gift my brother has for me today.

Please take me beyond my wanting to fix, so that I may see what he truly has to offer me.

Please show me the inner wisdom that comes, when I accept another simply for being where they are.

Show me the gift that another will show me about myself.

And there is one other gift that each person has to offer us. It is the gift of their divinity, of their being a child of God. When we are given the gift of finding the gift in everyone we are given the gift of seeing God.

Let me see Your clear reflection of Who I am.

Let me see You shining through my brothers' eyes.

Let me hear You speaking through my brothers' words.

Let me feel You in my brothers' presence.

Let me see Your light each time I look into another's heart.

Let me find the gift of You in everyone.

--Amen

THE GIFT OF FORGIVENESS

Forgiveness is something we have all struggled with in one situation or another. Ultimately, we would like to forgive, but we are afraid of what that might mean. We hold many fears, resentments, and much anger in our hearts. This we know hurts us, and truly seen we would like to let it all go. But, the biggest block to asking for forgiveness is the fear that what has happened to us before will happen to us again. Sometimes we keep anger because we fear that if we lose it, the same things may happen to us again, the same people may take advantage of us again, the same situations may occur again, the same feelings of helplessness may be activated again.

We keep resentments in order to remind us that we do not wish these occurrences in our lives anymore. Often we keep fear in our lives—"Lest we forget." Lest we forget, so that the things we fear may never happen again. Lest we be tricked by the same feelings, the same words, the same people.

We fear letting forgiveness in, because we fear it will dissolve our last lines of defense. This is quite true—forgiveness dissolves all our defenses. But what we must truly question is—do our defenses really keep us safe? Does keeping fear, resentment, and anger in our lives really keep us free from fear? Or do these defenses keep the very things we wish protection from? Is our focus protection, or is our focus on seeing another way?

The gift of Forgiveness does not require us to condone anything that has happened to us. It does not require us to accept what has caused us pain and despair. The gift of Forgiveness simply says—Let us go beyond all these things to see another way.

We are not kept safe by defenses, we can only see our choice, our strength, and the truth by seeing there is another way.

The gift of Forgiveness shows us another way of living. We forgive not what has been done to us—we forgive that anything could have been done to hurt the essence of our true being. The gift of Forgiveness takes us beyond our fear and puts us in touch with our strength, our choice.

The gift of Forgiveness shows that it is love and not protection that takes us beyond these occurrences ever happening again. Protection, by its very nature, is to keep, and what it keeps are the very fears we are trying to protect against. Forgiveness is to let go, for ultimately, we do not wish these patterns of anger, pain, and abuse in our lives any longer. We do not wish our anguish to continue. We forgive in order to let go of. We do not forgive in order to condone. We forgive in order to let go and be given another way.

It is difficult to see that keeping reminders of what we fear will not save us—it will only keep our patterns going in continuous, crazy circles.

The gift of Forgiveness promises another way. It is the promise of release. It is the promise of choice. It is the promise of remembrance, but this remembrance is of our innocence. This remembrance helps us see the innocence of those we have been trying to protect ourselves from. It does not whitewash. It does not sweep anything under the carpet. It simply says:

> *"Here is what I see was done to me, please help me see innocence beyond all this. Please show me that these people are not what they use. That beyond all the solutions that these people sought to control life with, they are not these solutions, and they are not these controls. Beyond everything, there is innocence. I can't see this—please show me that beyond everything, there is innocence. It is this that forgiveness will guide me to see."*

We repeat—forgiveness is a gift. We do not have to find it. We do not have to pretend it. It is a vision that heals all our perceptions of whatever has caused us pain, suffering, and misery. It is a vision that shows us who we truly are. It is a vision that shows us our true strength and completeness. It is a gift that guides us to another way beyond our patterns, beyond our situations, and beyond our protection.

Forgiveness is the pathway to seeing the light of love in ourselves and in others. It is the pathway to all healing. It is the pathway to seeing innocence. It is the pathway to freedom beyond all that has kept us suffering. It is the pathway to God's holy vision with which we may see and enter a world in all its purity, and all its love.

Question: Do I choose resentment so this will never happen again?

Answer: No, choose forgiveness, not so this thing will be prevented, but so it may be let go of forever.

Truly, when we forgive, we invite in healing. When we forgive someone we are saying: "I wish this person to be totally healed from all their illusions, all their controls, all their problems. I wish to see this person healed so that he or she, too, can be a loving, caring, and connected being of light." When we forgive a situation, we are inviting that situation to be used for healing. We are inviting all aspects of that situation to be healed so that only love, not pain, will remain.

Forgiveness is an invitation—for another way, for love, for healing, which includes all of us. When we are healed, when we are in touch with our wholeness and completeness—what indeed is there to forgive?

THE GIFT OF FREEDOM

We have been addicted to many things. Some of us have been addicted to substance, some of us have been addicted to relationships. Some of us have been addicted to pain and chaos. Still others of us have been addicted to work and accomplishment. Some of us have been addicted to pleasing and making others happy. And some of us have been addicted to almost everything. With all our addictions, we have not known freedom. But the biggest addiction of all has been the addiction to our way.

We have been addicted to having our world be as we think it should be, and it is this we have been imprisoned by. We are not free from the world of our making, for it is what we have made with our own determination to control that keeps us prisoners.

We cannot have freedom from something, for freedom is not an escape.

The gift of freedom gives us what is already ours. In giving our biases over to the care of our Higher Power, we will at last know Freedom. True Freedom is not freedom to have our will be done, true Freedom is the gift of having "Thy Will be done."

The gift of Freedom goes beyond everything we have made to the true Freedom of our Higher Power's Will, Love, and Caring. We are free of our addiction and, by the grace of God, we are free to live a life of fullness and connection. We are free to live in peace and serenity. The past and the future have no hold on us any longer. We are free to be happy—now.

We do not have to fight for God's Freedom—it is a gift. We do not have to defend our freedom, for in defense we will always lose. We need only ask for the gift to be given.

Prayer:

Higher Power,

Let me be free in You.

Let me be free from all pain and desperation in You.

Let me be free to be all that I am—in You.

Let me be free to see the support of others in Your loving care.

Please give me the gift of Your Freedom, so I may set others free.

--Amen

THE GIFT OF FUN

We have often confused gratification with fun. We have sought desperately after pleasure and we have called this fun. Very often this pursuit of fun did not bring us any joy, but we pursued it anyway, hoping to gratify our desperate thirst within.

We know we were supposed to have fun, but fun seemed to be a huge pretence that we all entered into to hide our despair. The search for fun was an escape from the grim controls that seized us. We pretended to have fun. We tried desperately to have fun, but most often this pursuit only emphasized the separation we felt and the loneliness inside.

The gift of fun is the gift of joining. We join with others in the freedom of expressing who we are. We join in the moment simply to share our joy, our being together.

With the gift of fun, all pretence is gone for we may laugh at our desperation and our controls, knowing that there is a gift of another way. The gift of fun is the gift that comes when we allow our Higher Power to look after all that has weighed us down and oppressed us. We give Him all our conflicts and difficulties and are given instead the gift of fun.

The gift of fun comes with the gift of acceptance—acceptance of ourselves and acceptance of others. We no longer have to take ourselves so seriously, for our burden of having to manage the world and everyone in it is gone.

The gift of fun is the gift of our lightness of being. We are not trying to fit in any longer, for we know it is our Higher Power that holds our place for us in all situations. We cannot make fun, try to have fun or pretend to have fun—it is a gift. It is the gift of the child within us, totally loving, totally accepting, and totally wishing to share.

The gift of fun is our deep desire to share with others the beautiful gift of who we are. There is laughter in this gift for who we are, for who we really are, can bring only joy to those in our lives.

> *"Give me your responsibilities, your burdens, your cares, and I will give you joy in living—I will give you the gift of fun."*

THE GIFT OF GOING BEYOND ALL ILLUSIONS

Anything that blocks or keeps the gifts from us is an illusion. Anything that tells us we are not ultimately lovable and worthy is an illusion. Anything that keeps us separate and alone is an illusion. Anything that blocks love's awareness from us is an illusion. Anything that insists on pain and conflict is an illusion. Anything that disconnects us from our Source is an illusion.

This is not to deny how we feel, this is not to pretend that we don't see what we see. This is not to put down our experience of what has seemed to happen to us. It is only to say we may see through these things to acknowledge that there must be another way, and with this acknowledgment we may ask to go beyond each and every fearful thought, feeling, and experience. We acknowledge how we feel, what we see, and what appears to be happening. But, if this is bringing us pain, we may wish another way, we may wish the reality of God's Love, Peace and Healing instead.

One thing about illusion is simply this—it never changes. We are not given the gift of Reality in order to make our illusions more comfortable. What is real is real, and what is illusion is illusion. We cannot marry the two. We cannot bring the two together.

When we come from fear, the feelings, the experience is always the same. When we come from peace, the connections, the miracles always occur.

When we get discouraged, when we are experiencing the same feelings and circumstances, we are asked to remember—"There is a gift that goes beyond all illusions. And if I am feeling separate and alone, I am experiencing the illusion that my Source is not within and all around me."

Truly, all illusion is a failure to recognize each moment Who walks beside us and what gifts He carries.

Illusion, then, is not seeing that we are one with each other, one with ourselves, and one with God.

No, illusions don't change. You will not be able to make them real. The illusion of rejection does not change. It contains the same hopelessness and despair. The illusion of finding our own solutions with our own willpower never changes. It contains the same competitiveness, desperation, and alienation, as it always will. The illusion that we are alone and no one cares still contains the same pain and helplessness as it always has. The illusion that our way can make us happy still carries the same desperate search, the same feelings of emptiness that never find satisfaction or fulfillment.

The gift of going beyond all illusions simply has us recognize that we are in illusion any time we do not feel the Love, the Ease and the Support that is all around us. Again, it is not to deny the illusion; it is not to feel guilty for experiencing the illusion—it is to consider: "This may not have to be. I no longer wish this to be my reality. I wish the reality of God's Truth, God's Vision, and God's Healing instead. I wish to go beyond this illusion."

The gift of going beyond illusions is the gift of asking for another vision—for God's reality. The gift of going beyond all illusion puts us in touch with the reality that there is always another way that includes everyone's well-being and healing. It is a reality that contains all the gifts. It is a reality that includes everyone in its healing presence. It is a reality that shows our wholeness, our strength, and our connection with the Source of all that is real, supportive, and caring.

This reality cannot be changed. With this gift we are put in touch with that which is changeless. We go beyond illusion to truth—the truth of love that can heal any situation. The truth of forgiveness which allows us to be free. The truth of understanding which allows us to let go of whatever has brought us pain. The truth of joy which is forever present and unconquerable. We go beyond illusion to come Home.

The end of all dreaming is the awakening to peace.

THE GIFT OF GOING BEYOND CONTROLOHOLISM

We use controls, because ultimately we fear to let go. We try to control things because we cannot see our safety and happiness coming any other way. We are like little children hiding in the dark, afraid to come to the light. And in our fears we keep the darkness and do everything not to let the light in.

We stand at the threshold of letting go and it feels like death. All we have controlled to this point, all we thought we must do to stay alive, all we thought we must do to keep sane is asked to be let go of. We are terrified. The expression: "You have to die to gain life" is very appropriate here, for it is the death of all that we have tried to control.

It is like facing the deepest black hole, which seems to consume everything. It seems like a vortex from which nothing escapes. This is what letting go of controls feels like to many of us.

All of our lives when we felt the vortex approaching, when we felt the call to let go coming, we tried to frantically swim away using more and more of our controls to keep this "threat" at a distance. "Ask me anything, but don't ask me to let go!"

We have become very inventive in holding on to our controls, but the natural flow of the universe still draws us to the point of letting go. With white knuckles we hang on to and try to reinforce what we think saves us. Letting go, itself, is seen as an invitation to let in terror and insanity.

We have become very tired and very fearful in our struggle to control our lives. We are like scared little children, unable to see safety anywhere except in what we are holding on to so desperately.

We have fought letting go. We have resisted letting go. But most of all we have been afraid to let go.

The gift of going beyond controloholism is the gift of being taken gently through the vortex and out into the Light. The gift of going beyond controloholism is being led through "the valley of the shadow of death" into Life Eternal. For we finally see there is no vortex, it is only our fear and resistance that we have been fighting. There is only Light—the Light of our Higher Power. Beyond what we control is our Higher Power waiting with open arms to give us all solutions, to give us all comfort and care. There is no valley of the shadow of death—it is only our fearful imaginings in the dark where we haven't allowed the light in. There are no shadows in God's Light.

The gift of going beyond controloholism is the gift of letting go in order to come into the Light. Nothing will be taken from us, but our fears will go as, one by one, we let go of what we have tried to control and see that what we have tried to control, has controlled us.

We have tried to control our safety and have made letting go into the deepest vortex, into the blackest black hole. We have tried to control our fears and they have grown in the darkness of our control. We have tried to control staying alive and have faced the spectre of death constantly. With our controls we have feared life, for life cannot be controlled without blocking its light.

The gift of going beyond controloholism is the gift of seeing that the deep vortex becomes a tiny ripple that we gently flow over.

The gift of going beyond controloholism is the gift that shows our blackest black hole becoming filled with Light when we finally are given the courage to look into it.

The way out is the way through. We have been swimming away from our Higher Power, and the insanity of our controls is that we have made our Higher Power into something fearful.

We let go, not in order to die, but to gain Life.

We let go, because in our darkness we see that our controls don't save us—they only keep the Light from us.

The gift of going beyond controloholism is the gift of going beyond all our controls into the heart of the vortex that will lead us Home.

Our Higher Power is waiting in what appears to be the depths of the vortex to show us there is only the gentle flow of His Care. Our Higher Power is waiting in the depths of the deepest black hole to show us the Light that always surrounds us.

The gift of going beyond controloholism is the gift of letting go. It is a gift that will take us beyond our fears to the safety we have sought for so desperately and so longingly. Let go and He will take you beyond...

THE GIFT OF GOING BEYOND JUDGMENT

Who are we to judge? Once this is realized, we are ready to receive the gift of going beyond all judgment. What we judge we have condemned and in that condemnation is our own sentence of guilt.

The gift of going beyond judgment is really the gift of being released of all fear, for we judge what we fear and in that judgment is fear perpetuated.

In our relentless judgment of others we lose sight of the fact that it is truly us that we judge. With the gift of going beyond all judgment, we see the connectedness of everything. We see our gifts; we see the gift of each other. For how can we receive gifts when we are constantly judging what is given us?

Judgment has nothing to do with choice, for when we judge we will not see all our solutions.

The gift of going beyond all judgment allows us to receive all gifts, all solutions, and all support. How can we truly see someone we have judged—how can we see the gift they would bring us?

The gift of going beyond all judgment sets us free, for no longer do we have to judge and condemn our own being—"Who am I to judge Who I am?" God's only judgment is the judgment of innocence. This is the gift that waits beyond all judgment. Beyond all judgment we will find the gift of our own innocence and of our brother's innocence. When we no longer have to judge, we are free. Judgment is a mighty barrier to all gifts our Higher Power would give us each day.

Just for today, I do not have to judge myself and my actions. I may ask to be guided in the most loving way.

Just for today, I do not have to judge anyone else and their actions. I may instead ask to see their gift to me.

Just for today, I do not have to judge what is occurring in my life. I need not judge where I am nor where I should be. I may ask instead for all that is happening to be used for my healing.

Just for today, I will ask not to condemn, but to forgive.

Just for today, there will be acceptance, peace and innocence–beyond all my judgments.

THE GIFT OF GRACE

It is often said: "By the grace of God..." Grace is the state of leaving the past totally forgiven and totally free. With the gift of Grace, we are given a new beginning; we are allowed to begin anew a life, not run by our selfish ways, but a life given to us each day by a Power greater than ourselves. Grace, then, is the state where we always have the opportunity, the choice, to come Home to God once again.

The gift of Grace is that gift that allows us to come Home no matter what we have thought, done, or been. The slate is wiped clean by the gift of God's Grace, and we may claim our innocence once more. The gift of Grace washes us clean with the Truth of Who we truly are. Grace allows the past to disappear and the future to be held in trust—our Higher Power's Trust.

By the Grace of God we are set free from everything that has enslaved us and all that we have sought to imprison. It is the gift that releases all our desperations and addictions so we may walk free once more. The gift of Grace is indeed amazing, for with this gift all that has held us slips away and we are born anew to the freshness of our being. We are given a new life—by the Grace of God.

With Grace we rise above our fears and see them fade into nothingness. By the Grace of God all guilt is washed clean and we see our own gifts with this moment of beginning again. With Grace are we given another way. With Grace are we released, and with Grace we begin again each new day. By the Grace of God the past is let go and we meet ourselves now, totally forgiven, and forever innocent.

The power of Grace to forgive all "sins" is immense, for with the gift of Grace, we only see the light of who we and all others are.

With God's Grace is all forgiveness possible, for God's Grace will ultimately show us there is nothing to forgive.

THE GIFT OF GRATITUDE

The Gift of Gratitude is the gift which holds the key to all of God's Gifts, for it is in the state of Gratitude that we are aware of what is truly given. Gratitude is the great opener to all gifts. It is the gift that opens us to the awareness of our Higher Power's Will for us. It is the gift in which answers are heard and solutions can be given. Only in gratitude can we recognize what our gifts are. Gratitude, like all gifts of God, is the gift of the heart. It puts us in touch with the heart of the matter.

We do not have to try to be grateful—it is a gift. We do not have to pretend to be grateful—gratitude is given. It is a gift that connects us immediately with our Higher Power's Love. It is a gift with which we will recognize all other gifts.

"What can you be grateful for?", is the entrance to all healing. It is the gift of inclusion where we feel connected with Life again. It is the great heart opener. It is the great catalyst for letting go and it is what we will feel when we give everything to our Higher Power.

There is a deep endless well of gratitude that we are given once we ask: "What can I be grateful for?" The gift of gratitude is the gift that will open us to all miracles, all healing, and our Higher Power's Will for us each moment.

THE GIFT OF GUIDANCE

There is some confusion about guidance. We often wonder if it's guidance or wishful thinking. Sometimes we ask for guidance and do not feel it forthcoming. Sometimes we receive guidance and doubt its truth—is it our Higher Power speaking or simply our self-will trying to control once again?

We do not know how to tell what is guidance and what is ego. This is a simple truth. Not only can we not manage our own lives, we cannot manage whatever guidance comes to us. This, too, we must give to our Higher Power and ask for His gift of Guidance.

We ask our Higher Power to be the guidance in our lives. If we are in the way, we ask our Higher Power to even use this for healing.

There is much fear surrounding guidance. We fear we will not hear it. We fear we may be imagining it. We fear it may come from an inappropriate source. How can we tell what is true guidance? Very simply—we can't. The gift of Guidance is given because by ourselves we are without direction. We ask our Higher Power to be the Source of the Guidance, the Truth of the Guidance and the Keeper of the Guidance. We, by ourselves, cannot verify Truth, nor can we defend it. The gift of Guidance is given when we admit we are without guidance and cannot distinguish our own management from what is true. Very simply—the gift of Guidance is the admittance that we don't know, but our Higher Power does.

Prayer:

**God, would You look after my guidance
and guide me to what is wholly true, wholly
loving, and wholly joyous.**

Would You guide me in Your care.

Would You guide me to see forgiveness and innocence in everyone.

Would You always guide me to choose honesty and healing.

Would You guide me to be open and accepting of myself and others.

Would You guide me to see beauty and wonder.

Would You guide me in the integrity of my being.

Would You guide me in gratitude for all I have to give and all I have been given.

Would You guide me to walk in Your light, surrounded by Your Peace.

Would You guide me to always choose Your gift of Guidance.

Would You be the Guidance that guides me to You.

--Amen

THE GIFT OF HARMONY

There is a harmony that is eternally present amongst all beings. The gift of Harmony shows us what is already present but what is continually obscured by our own controls and manipulations.

We have many strange beliefs about other living beings. We believe we are better than other species, and even our own species has certain beings that we feel superior to. We feel the universe needs our supervision, needs our fixing. We feel certain situations need to be manipulated or directed to go a certain way. We feel those in our lives could stand some improvement, some readjustment to make them better people. We are continually trying to fix or change ourselves to fit some image we think would make us happy. The result has been that we have been fighting nature, each other, and ourselves. And with each thing that we "fix", somehow the problem becomes more and more discordant.

The gift of Harmony is an amazing gift. It is an amazing gift because it shows us—nothing needs to be fixed. There is an inherent divine nature in everything that, when truly allowed to express itself, is in harmony with all other things.

The gift of Harmony shows us that what is not in harmony cannot be brought to this awareness by our control. We ask for the gift of Harmony to enter each situation where there is conflict and discord. We ask for the gift of Harmony to bring that tremendous awareness of letting others be. This gift does not ignore disharmony—it acknowledges that somewhere in our management, we have lost sight of this gift.

This gift does not mean anything cannot be changed. It means that what is changed is in harmony with everyone's well-being and everything's well-being. It means that the gift of Harmony is what changes each situation of conflict.

The gift of Harmony puts us in touch with our own center of being so we may see the divinity in each thing around us. Truly, the gift of Harmony is seeing God expressing Himself through everything. God becomes an expression of our being and we allow God to express in the most appropriate way through all areas, through all people, and through all situations in our lives.

Harmony is God expressing through trees, mountains, rivers, animals, friends, family, events, thoughts, feelings, being.

The gift of Harmony is also the gift of simplicity. It is so simple when we allow God to be the harmony. It is so simple when we allow the wisdom of God to work through all situations and all beings. There is such a gift in each living thing—to see this is to see Harmony. To try to fix this, is to see nothing of any value.

Gratitude for all of nature, for all of life, will bring us in harmony with ourselves, and with the world. There can be no harmony if we are not at peace or in harmony with our own being.

The gift of Harmony allows us to see our own part in the divine plan and that part is total appreciation of all gifts.

God is the harmony with which all conflict, all discord, is simply resolved.

The gift of Harmony is the awareness of the symphony of living, of connecting, of expressing with everything around us. It is the gift of being part of everything and it is the gift of seeing everything within us. It is the gift of Oneness—living in peace, living in appreciation, living in wisdom, living in respect, living in harmony.

We are not in charge of the orchestra. That is why there has been much discord. We are an integral part of the orchestra. But, our Higher Power is the Conductor that harmonizes everyone in the expression of their true beauty and being.

THE GIFT OF HAVING ALL MISTAKES FORGIVEN (MERCY)

Really, the only mistake we make is thinking we can run our lives without the help of our Higher Power. The mistake is that we put everything ahead of choosing God. We think we can do things alone. We think we can manage. We forget to ask for our Higher Power to be our lives.

Coming from management, we all make mistakes—it is inevitable. We are walking without the light of our Higher Power. We are acting without the awareness of our inner knowing, without our Higher Power's direction. We are being in separation, and our being is out of touch with our Self. We are with each other without asking for our Higher Power's love and understanding. We are separate from ourselves and from each other. We make the mistake of choosing to be separate from God.

The gift of having all mistakes forgiven does not make us guilty. It only recognizes we have been managing our lives and have not turned our lives over to our Higher Power's care. We do not admit our mistakes to be condemned and judged for them, we admit them into the light so our Higher Power may gently correct them and show us another way. If we do not experience peace, we have been mistaken. If there is not an abundance of love in our lives, we have been mistaken. If we are not at Ease, we have been mistaken. If we do not see the innocence of others, we have been mistaken. If we feel fear and pain, we have been mistaken.

It is not to judge our mistakes; it is simply time to admit them, to let them go, to release them. It is not to avoid making mistakes; it is to realize what is not working in our lives, what is not healing in our lives, what is not loving in our lives. We may see our mistakes and ask, "What would I like to see instead of this? How would I like to feel? What would I like to happen?" We are not our mistakes, but hiding our mistakes will blind us to all the gifts that are given.

The gift of having all mistakes forgiven is the gift of realizing there is no mistake we cannot give to our Higher Power to receive His blessing and forgiveness instead. This gift calls us Home beyond all mistakes to receive the gift of innocence, the gift of acceptance.

The gift of having all mistakes forgiven is the gift of Mercy. The gift of Mercy sees the origin of our mistakes and simply says:

> *"Come Home, all is forgiven."*

The gift of having all of our mistakes forgiven, the gift of Mercy, is the gift of coming Home once again—totally free, totally pure, and totally innocent. We may begin again. And each mistake we have ever made, we may give to our Higher Power and say:

Prayer:

Would You take this mistake and even use this for healing.

Would You mend what I have broken.

Would You open what I have shut out.

Would You bring love where I have brought judgment and pain.

Would You bring together whatever relationships I have torn apart and would You teach me how to live in acceptance and understanding.

Would You take whatever I have made or done, and in Your wisdom correct it so I may let in all of Your love, all of Your mercy, all of Your gifts.

--Amen

The gift of having all mistakes forgiven is the gift of God's Mercy. There is no punishment in His Mercy, there is no retribution, there is no penance. There is only acceptance and love, for the only mistake we have ever truly made is the mistake of living without God.

We may accept this merciful gift for ourselves, and in this acceptance we may extend Mercy to others. What a wonderful gift to give, for we have all condemned ourselves for mistakes we have made. We have carried the belief that we were a mistake. We have carried the mistakes of generations before us. But the gift of Mercy forgives **all** of our mistakes. It makes no distinction; it simply says:

> *"Bring your mistakes to Me."*

Instead of resentment, we may ask to give the gift of Mercy. Instead of condemnation, we may ask to give the gift of Mercy. We are merciful because we have received the gift of Mercy in our lives, and we are free. Who would not have Mercy to give to others when all mistakes have been forgiven? By God's Mercy we are free. By God's Mercy we are forgiven. By God's Mercy we may begin again, in all our innocence.

THE GIFT OF HAVING ALL QUESTIONS ANSWERED

We were often told not to question. We were told that we had to believe and that we could not question anything. We were told our faith depended upon an unquestioning loyalty to what we were taught. Not only was questioning not encouraged in most areas, but especially in matters of religion, questioning could amount to being a sin. It was simply not safe to question.

Often, we were afraid of asking questions out of a fear they would reveal our ignorance. We were afraid of being seen as slow or stupid. We were afraid that our questions would reveal to everyone that we did not know—we did not know how; we did not know why; we did not know what to do; we did not know how to be.

Often, we did not know what the question was. We did not have words for our doubts and our concerns. We simply felt uneasy and at a loss. We did not know what we wanted to ask.

The questions that we did ask never seemed to have a satisfactory answer. The deep thirst within us was not quenched by the answers others gave us. These answers only led to more questions that in turn weren't answered.

We often felt our questions were not answered with integrity and honesty. We were given a cover-up and a reality that did not strike the truth within us. We still wanted to know, but we were frustrated with the feeling that our questions would never be answered.

The gift of having all questions answered is, first of all, the freedom to doubt and question everything. Only by seeing that our Higher Power's truth can withstand all our questions will we be able to truly receive the answer. We will find that it is okay to question. We will find there are no "dumb" questions. We will find the gift of being able to bring all our questions to our Higher Power for His loving answers. We will find that it is not a sin to question—it is a gift.

The gift of having all questions answered is, ultimately, the gift of having our Higher Power be the answer to all our questions. It is in Him that all questions are answered. It is in Him that we will be answered with all honesty and all truth.

The gift of having all questions answered is the gift of seeing all the answers within us. It is the gift of being in touch with the awareness of these answers each time we have a question.

The gift of having all questions answered is the gift of having our questions touched by the Truth of what is already within us. The answers to our questions will quench that thirst and reflect our inner knowing. Our Higher Power's answers will connect to the knowledge of honesty and clarity that we have always wanted to connect with; the answers we have invariably always known.

The gift of having all questions answered is truly the gift of being reconnected with what has always been within us, to a loving God that will allow us to express and remember this truth.

Ultimately, all questions are "How may I be with You?" and once we ask this question, truly we are answered and all our questions will be no more, for we have been reconnected with our Source.

Prayer:

Dear God,

Would You give me the questions to ask so You may be my answer.

Would You show me it is okay to question everything.

Would You show me that You are the answer in which all questions, all doubts, disappear.

Would You be the Truth with which I am answered.

Would You be the Honesty with which I am answered.

Would You be the Knowing that quenches my thirst.

Would You be the Certainty that brings me in touch with Your Love.

Would You be the Wisdom with which I may see the gifts in all Your answers.

Would You be the answer of Love.

Would You be the answer of Connection.

Would You be the answer in which all my questions are answered in You.

--Amen

THE GIFT OF HAVING ALL THE TIME THERE IS—NOW

To be in the moment is not to keep out the past, nor the future—it is to allow time to go through the moment so that it is no longer resisted.

We do not experience the moment by shutting out time; we experience the moment by allowing time in.

Everything is allowed in the moment so that only what is real remains.

To go beyond time we do not protect, nor do we try to make time.

We allow time to come through, so we may have all the time there is. That moment of allowing time through and having all the time there is, is really the gift of being in the moment. This gift is received by allowing time to go through us rather than resisting it or trying to keep it.

What we resist becomes conflict and consequently our enemy. What we allow through is released and allows us to go beyond the time we are trying so desperately to overcome.

We never seem to have enough time because we would try to keep it. We would try to keep moments rather than allowing them through. We never seem to have enough time because we resist it. We resist the time that seems to change and age us. We try to keep where we are or we resist the time it takes to be where we want to be. We have made time an enemy, and we have tried to make time a prisoner. We have tried to protect time and we have sought to isolate and pin it down in a million different ways. We have sought to control time with our schedules and appointments. We have tried to hurry time with our routines and impatience. And we have sought to hold it back with all our aids to beauty and youth. We have sought to recapture time with entertainment and re-creation.

We have indeed sought to control time, and with this control have set up a mighty resistance.

The gift of having all the time there is allows time to come through without judgment and without control. We can only be in touch with all the time there is—Now. The moment is all eternity and the moment gives us the gift of all the time there is.

We allow time through. There is no need to stop it, keep it, hold it back, hurry it up, or control it in any way. When we give up the resistance to time, we have the gift of all the time there is, for we have the gift of the moment.

We don't keep out time to have moments. We allow all time in to see there is only the moment.

A moment is not to be protected. It is that instant when we have not sought to keep anything out and have been in touch with the fullness of that moment.

We don't put time on hold to have a moment; we allow time through so that only the moment remains.

Anytime we try to control time, it sets up a resistance and time becomes our enemy rather than the river with which we flow.

We don't make a moment—we allow it.

We don't make love—we allow it.

Ultimately, when we try to control the moment—we become lost in time. We become lost in past and future.

To have the gift of all the time there is, we must be willing to give up our control of time so we may go beyond it.

THE GIFT OF HEALING

It is perhaps simpler to look at healing if we look at the gifts connected with it. Each gift is a gift of healing.

With healing there comes the gift of Expression. To express is to heal. Each time, through judgment, through misunderstanding, we fail to express what we feel, what we are, we block the natural flow of the Life Energy. Disease, then, is lack of expression. We are somehow de-pressing the expression of our Higher Being. What we judge, we will not express. And what we judge does not let healing occur. We are not speaking of expression simply for the sake of expression. We are speaking of the Gift of Expression which allows us to share where we are really coming from and which allows us to express our innermost honesty, feelings and desires.

Another gift which comes with the gift of healing is the gift of being able to feel whatever needs to be felt. This is very connected with the gift of Expression. It is often said that what we feel can be healed. Blocking any feelings blocks the Life Energy that flows through us. We feel in order to heal. It is not a focussing on feelings so much as an allowing of feeling. We allow God or the Life Energy through in order to dissolve all feelings that have caused us pain.

The gift of Connection goes with healing. We find we need healing when we have disconnected from our Source. We find we need healing when, through old conclusions and judgments, we have disconnected from ourselves. To be separate is to be in need of healing, for truly, to heal is to join or connect with all that is around us once again. Healing is to connect with our innocence. It is to connect with the inner wisdom. It is to connect once again with our Worth as a Child of God.

Healing, then, is to invite all aspects of ourselves that we have judged, condemned, and cast off to come together in acceptance, understanding and love. All fragmented parts of ourselves are invited into the healing of the gift of Wholeness.

To heal is to bring in the gift of Light. We bring all doubts, all that we have kept separate and condemned, all that has been unsaid, unfelt, unseen, unheard, into the Light's awareness, and with this awareness all that has caused us pain may be released.

The gift of Connection brings acceptance of ourselves and acceptance of our place in being part of everything. We are reconnected with Who we are and what we have to offer.

With the gift of Healing, comes two more gifts—the gift of Nurturing and the gift of being able to receive. To appear to need healing is a sure sign that we have not allowed ourselves to be nurtured. We have kept out the Life Force that would envelop and care for us. We have judged ourselves as fragmented beings with some parts worthy of love, but most parts only worthy of punishment and banishment. Our being has become fragmented, and what we have judged as unworthy we have shut off from the Light. We have refused to let ourselves be fully nurtured.

What we judge, again, cannot be healed. What we judge we will not be able to receive healing for. To heal is to be able to receive. The gift of being able to receive gives us the tiny crack needed for healing to enter.

Truly, the gift of healing includes all the gifts to bring about the transformation from disease to ease. It may help us to say: To heal is to allow ourselves to be healed. This may seem obvious, but again we repeat that what we judge about ourselves we will not allow to be healed. And anything that we hold in judgment about another, we will refuse to let healing enter in our own lives.

The gift of coming from wherever we are coming from without judgment is a very important healing gift. To begin without judgment is to heal. To begin without judgment brings us to one of the most important gifts—Forgiveness.

Truly, forgiveness is not condoning, whitewashing, or having to accept whatever has happened to us. Forgiving is simply the desire, the asking, that another be healed. To desire healing for another, to want to see them healed, is forgiveness. To wish love for another, to desire that they find God's Love and God's Healing is forgiveness. And what we forgive in another, we forgive or heal in ourselves. To forgive ourselves is to invite healing in. To desire to see another healed of all their misperceptions is to invite all healing in.

To invite healing is to invite all of God's gifts. We may not know what healing is, but we may ask for each gift to come into our lives.

To heal is to feel.

To express is to heal.

To go beyond judgment is to heal.

To respect is to heal.

To receive is to heal.

To forgive is to heal.

To bless is to heal.

To be grateful is to heal.

To ask for trust is to heal.

To be nurtured is to heal.

To be able to doubt and question is to heal.

To share is to heal.

To open is to heal.

To be with God is to heal.

Truly, healing is all about gifts both in giving and receiving. Healing is to be One again. One with ourselves, one with each other, one with all things, one with God.

Prayer:

Holy Spirit, bring us together once more so we may see we are healed.

Bring our minds into oneness with Your Mind.

Bring our hearts together with Your Heart.

Bring our thoughts together with Your Love.

Bring Your Light so there is darkness no more.

Let us walk together in Oneness, so we can see our completeness, so we may see we are Healed in You.

--Amen

If we wish to heal both ourselves and others, one of the greatest gifts we may give is the gift of allowing all life to be. Allowing does not mean accepting illusion. Allowing means being in touch with the truth of all Life. We allow ourselves to truly be. We allow others to be, from the depths of our hearts, all that they can be. We allow with respect and we allow ourselves to live with respect. The gift of respect allows healing. We, as children of God, respect each other for who we truly are.

The gift of Asking is a most healing gift. To truly be able to ask is to heal. We have been unable to communicate with each other what is truly important in our hearts. We have not known how to ask, to share, to communicate. To truly ask and share with another is to heal, for listening and being heard reconnects us with the rest of ourselves. We are in each person. We are in each other. To heal is to recognize this once again.

The gift of being seen and heard is the recognition of ourselves in everything and in everyone. To heal is to be in touch with all that we are and we are everything.

The gift of healing, then, includes all gifts, for the gifts of God **are** our healing:

> **To heal is to go beyond our littleness, beyond our tiny ego mind to see our connection with all life.**
>
> **To heal is to be.**
>
> **To heal is to be in the moment.**
>
> **To heal is to ask for another way.**
>
> **To heal is to ask for Life, to ask for Love, to ask for all gifts, to ask for God.**
>
> **To heal is to bring our inner child Home where it is welcome and loved.**

To heal is to speak our hearts, and to hear the hearts of others.

To heal is to speak our truth and ask to see truth beyond all illusion.

To heal is to speak the language of love, for this is the only true connection.

To heal is to speak of our fears, for in the Light they lose all their power.

To heal is to speak about where we come from, for in this honesty there is nothing we cannot go beyond.

To heal is to speak of our difficulties in letting in healing, for in speaking of this, we may ask for another way.

To heal is to express our doubts, for these doubts may all be answered.

To heal we may speak of beginning and being a beginner, for in speaking of this our journey is complete.

To heal is to speak of acceptance, accepting that another may also find the way.

To heal is to call forth the God within, so we may speak with all respect, all understanding, and all love.

To heal is to let in. We may invite in, as part of our healing, all light, all love, all support, all possibilities, all solutions, all ease, all joy, all play, all being, all healing—all gifts.

THE GIFT OF HOLY ENCOUNTERS (OF THE JOYOUS KIND)

We have all wished to meet great masters of wisdom. We have wished to meet enlightened beings that would disclose to us all the seeming mysteries of the universe. We have wished to meet these great ones in order to experience a holy encounter.

These encounters are indeed a great gift. We experience those living in constant contact with themselves and with their Higher Power (Self). It is a great gift to be in the presence of those choosing to live in the spirit of God—to encounter those living and expressing the path of Peace.

This is indeed a holy encounter of the joyous kind, for we are shown the joy someone experiences when God is the center of their lives.

The gift of Holy Encounters would give even more than the encounter with "great masters". The greatest and holiest gift is to meet the Master in each one of us. We are not limited to the few who have attained enlightenment. The gift of Holy Encounters would exclude no one in its opportunity to see the holiness, to see the Spirit in each living thing.

What a truly wonderous and joyous gift to meet and encounter the Spirit in all that come into our lives.

Usually, we are busy judging the worth and value of each encounter. We judge how it serves us; what we can get out of it. We judge appearances, language, status, and even intelligence. But, the gift of Holy Encounters of the joyous kind does not judge, nor even suspend judgment. It simply says:

> *"Here is an opportunity to encounter holiness should I ask to go beyond all my judgments to receive this gift."*

The gift of Holy Encounters of the joyous kind is the most wonderous of gift exchanges. We are open to see the holiness of another revealed, and in exchange for this willingness, we will receive encounters that are both joyous, and holy.

There is nothing to master, but to ask to see the Master, to express the Master in all that we do.

Prayers:

I ask to see the Master and I am given my brother.

I ask to see the Master and I am given my own reflection.

I ask to see the Master and I am given an endless opportunity to see Him everywhere.

I ask to see the Master, and I am given the Master revealing Himself through all that He shows me, in all that I see.

Master, master my judgment so I may see You.

Master, master my condemnation so I may see me.

Master, master my fears so that I may see we all are the Master—we all express You.

Master, please reveal Yourself in all whom I encounter.

The Master is in you.

The Master is in me.

The Master is the bridge that unites our encounter.

The Master is the vision that makes our encounter holy.

The Master is the love that makes our encounter joyous.

--Amen

A Holy Encounter is one where we have no expectations or judgments—we are simply open to experience the innocence and the gift in our encounter.

THE GIFT OF HONESTY

Being honest has always seemed to take the form of a confession. We believed that when we were honest, we confessed our sins and then we were punished for them. It has not seemed safe to be honest, for honesty reveals our vulnerability, our controls, our manipulations, our fears, our insecurity, and our desperation. We have spent a whole lifetime trying to hide these very things. At times we have tried to be honest, but we have felt that those around us either ridiculed or tried to suppress this honesty. They too, it seemed, were afraid of the vulnerability, the exposure that honesty brought. Honesty seemed to be a witch-hunt where we looked for our defects only to condemn them and judge ourselves for having them.

The gift of Honesty is somewhat different than the honesty we are used to. The gift of Honesty is our release from hell. The admittance of Honesty is the gateway to our release, to our freedom. The gift of Honesty allows admittance—admittance of and admittance to. We admit what we try to control so we may find admittance to a newfound freedom. The gift of Honesty allows the caring person we really are to shine forth from all we have sought to hide and control.

The gift of Honesty is the courage to express and feel that vulnerability we have sought so desperately to hide. Honesty and vulnerability go hand in hand, so it is no wonder we have been tremendously reluctant to ask for this gift. To express how we truly feel, to share where we are coming from, to be what we are guided to be, and to say what we need to say, puts us in a position of vulnerability. The gift of Honesty shows us that ultimately the only thing we are vulnerable to is what we have made through our own self-will. We are vulnerable to losing what we are trying to control. We are vulnerable to losing the image we have tried to create. We are vulnerable to losing the mask, which we hide behind.

To receive the gift of Honesty is indeed to be vulnerable, not to hurt, but to losing our self-will. It is sometimes difficult to explain to someone that being vulnerable in our honesty brings tremendous safety and strength. We have been taught that the opposite is true.

But we must remember, Honesty is a gift, given to us whenever it is appropriate for us to come clean and to share. It is a gift that allows us to be without having to judge that being. It is a gift that allows us to say: "I don't know," and to ask for Knowing. It is a gift that allows us to speak what is in our hearts in order to receive healing.

We are honest, not in order to find confession, but in order to gain admittance to another way of living. We ask for this gift so we may finally see our innocence. We ask for this gift so that each time we are caught up in our addictions, we may admit it and ask for another way. We ask for this gift so we may finally come from wherever we hide into the light of acceptance.

Prayer:

God, would You be the Honesty with which I share whatever needs to be done or said in any situation.

Would You give me the Honesty to simply be.

Would You give me the Honesty to admit when I'm trying to control or manage a situation.

Would You give me the Honesty to share wherever I am coming from, if it is appropriate to do so.

Would You give me the Honesty to let others see me.

Would You give me the Honesty to admit when I don't know how.

Would You give me the Honesty to come from behind any pretense, to come to the heart of the matter.

Would You give me the Honesty to live in Your Care— one day at a time.

Would You Be the Honesty with which I live.

--Amen

THE GIFT OF HUMILITY

The gift of Humility is not a humiliation, for who would offer humiliation as a gift? Humility is a gift because it enables us to ask. There is no humiliation in having to ask for assistance. There is no humiliation in asking for God's help, for God's care and for God's understanding.

The gift of Humility enables us to see that we cannot go it alone, we need the love of others, we need the love of a Higher Power.

The gift of Humility is a recognition that our ways and our solutions have not worked. It is a recognition that we must give up our solutions in order to find healing.

The gift of Humility does not judge where we are, it is a happy celebration that we are finally asking for God's support and care.

This gift celebrates our readiness to allow another way.

Humiliation occurs when we find our goals and our ways do not work. We are humiliated in the defeat of our way. But the gift of Humility is not a part of this defeat, nor does it judge what we have tried to hang on to. It recognizes that we are not defeated—we are finally ready to accept the support and wisdom of all things. We may recognize that our way does not work and with the gift of Humility we may see this as a blessing and as an entrance to a greater strength, a greater understanding, a greater knowing.

Humility is indeed a great gift, for it allows strength where we have admitted our weakness. It allows faith where our doubts have become too much for us. It broadens our awareness where we have been stuck in the ego's limited vision. It allows us to begin again where we have been struggling in our ceaseless patterns. It allows us to ask where we have thought we had to do it ourselves. It allows us to receive where we have thought that we had to come up with the answers. It allows us to be real where we have sought to impress and maintain an image. It allows us to admit our mistakes and to ask for a better way. It allows complete forgiveness, for with the gift of humility, we see we are in no position to judge.

The gift of Humility enables us to listen and hear the answers that will guide us in a true and loving direction. With humility we are reachable and we are teachable.

The gift of Humility allows us to see our innocence by seeing that we need to ask—our ways have not worked, our vision has not seen, our strength has been weak, our love has been conditional. In the midst of our despair we are offered the gift of Humility—a gift that simply invites us to ask for the strength and love of our Higher Power.

Our Higher Power never demands our humiliation—humiliation is what we have created. Our Higher Power offers us the gift of Humility, a gift which invites us to ask for our Higher Power's help in all that we do.

Humiliation is a lack of respect for who we are. Humility offers respect to others, to our Higher Power and to ourselves. With the eyes of humility all is seen with compassion, understanding, respect and love. It is a gift that allows us to see the preciousness of all beings and the preciousness of our new beginning.

THE GIFT OF INCLUSION

A gift is not a gift unless all are included in its blessing. In other words, love is not love unless everyone is included in receiving this gift. A solution is not a solution unless it is for everyone's well-being. Forgiveness is not forgiveness unless all things are included in its light.

Truly, the gift of Inclusion means that there are no conditions on any of God's gifts. The gift of Inclusion means we are one together and each gift is for all of us—for all beings.

It is amazing how many times we do not include ourselves in the receiving of gifts. We put ourselves last on the list and determine that if there is enough to go around, we will accept some for ourselves. We determine that we cannot be happy until everyone is happy. We determine we cannot let go of pain and resentment until everyone has let go. We determine we cannot share until everyone else has gone first with their sharing. Often, in this arrangement, we don't allow ourselves to receive the gift of Happiness, the gift of Release, the gift of Sharing.

The gift of Inclusion does not deal in line-ups. It does not deal in turns; it does not deal in order. It simply states that all are entitled to all of God's gifts. It does not say that anyone should be first, nor does it demand that anyone go last. It simply says—ask to receive God's gifts, now.

The wonderful thing about God's gifts is that receiving them does not take anything away from anyone else. Receiving God's gifts only enhances the possibility of others asking for and receiving the gifts that are theirs.

We are asked to include ourselves in receiving each gift that is held for us. We are asked to see that everything is included in the gift of God's Grace.

Prayer:

Where there is a solution, let it include me.

Where there is love, let me open to receive it.

Where there is joy, let me include myself in its presence.

Where there is sharing, let me give all that I am.

Where there is support, let me include myself in its comfort.

Where there is acceptance, let me be in its center.

Where there is patience, let me receive this gift for my own journey.

Where there is an answer, let it include everyone.

Where there is light, let me be its shining.

Where there is Inclusion, let me see that I am included in the very heart of its connection.

Please include me in all Your plans, all Your direction, and all Your Love.

Would You be the inclusion with which I am included in the oneness of Life.

Please help me to include others in the light of Your forgiveness.

Please help me to include everyone in my prayers for healing.

Please help me to include You in my Life.

--Amen

THE GIFT OF INNOCENCE

We have had a strange belief that our innocence could be lost. We sometimes long for the times when we felt pure and innocent. Some us of can't even remember this feeling. Many times we feel ugly and tainted. We feel guilty. We feel something is wrong with us. We feel full of shame. We even feel sinful.

We look around and judge those we see. We see them guilty of various acts and omissions. We see with eyes of condemnation and judgment.

When we feel we have lost our innocence, we lose sight of our worth, for how can someone so evil be worthy of anything? And when we see others, we do not see them as innocent because we do not see our own gift of Innocence. We see the many "wrongs" that they are doing. We see their mistakes. We see their guilt. So deep is the conviction of our "original sin" of being bad, of being wrong, that the mere mention of seeing innocence seems like a lie.

We often don't want to see the possibility of innocence, for we think that means letting someone off the hook, letting them go without punishment so that they may hurt us all over again.

Quite often we do not wish to hear of our own innocence, for innocence has been mistakenly connected with being naive, with being gullible. And if there is one thing we do not wish to be, it is to be gullible or taken in by anyone.

The gift of Innocence is one gift we have refused to receive more than any other gift.

Let us consider the gift of Innocence. Innocence has full awareness. It does not see some things and not others. It sees everything about everyone. It does not pretend. It does not whitewash. It does not deny. What the gift of Innocence does do is to see our true nature beyond all that we have said, thought, or done. Innocence, in full awareness, accepts that we are not our beliefs, conclusions, deformities, or insane thinking. It sees the truth of who we are beyond what we have made or anything we have been using.

The gift of Innocence does not deny what it sees. It recognizes:

> *This is not who you are. You are not anger. You are not hate. You are not fear, and you are not evil. You have been mistaken—beyond all these things, you are innocent.*

The gift of Innocence and the gift of our Inner child are inseparable, for truly, it is only with the gift of our inner child, it is only with the vision of the child, that innocence can be seen. In each of us there is a child, wishing for acceptance and love. Beyond all our commotions, retaliations, attacks, and defenses there is a child asking...

> *"Do you love me? I'm afraid the answer will be, 'no'."*

The gift of Innocence is an incredibly powerful gift, for it has the power to transform what we see as evil into the heart of a child. It has the power to transform hate into love and acceptance. It has the power to transform all attacks into outstretched arms, welcoming each other Home. It has the power to take us beyond each and every illusion that we ever had about ourselves and show us the radiant soul within us, the loving heart that is our original nature.

The gift of Innocence is the great dissolver of all pain. For what is pain but the misguided thought that we are guilty and surrounded by those wishing to punish us for this.

We are so afraid of this gift, for we still believe we are innocent until proven guilty. And so we wait in fear until someone discovers the guilt that is surely within us.

But the gift of Innocence sees all our belief in guilt, all our belief in evil and says: "No, you are mistaken, I see only innocence—that is all that is within you."

The gift of Innocence is the gift of Who we are. It is the only gift that will truly teach us about ourselves. It is the only thing to learn about each other. It is the only thing to see, and it is the only thing to heal our dreams of guilt.

When you let me see your fears—I see
your innocence.

When you open and share your vulnerability—
I see your innocence.

When you admit you do not know and reach
out to me—I see your innocence.

When you are crying and tell me you are too
afraid to open—I see your innocence.

When you are at a loss for words and can only
feel—I see your innocence.

When you are honest and take a chance to tell
me how you really feel—I see your innocence.

When you are joyful and light-hearted and
cannot help but share these gifts with
everyone—I see your innocence.

When you start from wherever you are with the
willingness to let go—I see your innocence.

When you say, "God, help me, I'm going crazy!"—I see your innocence.

When you are sitting there looking and feeling guilty—I see your innocence.

When you let me see all of you—I see your innocence.

This is easy for me to say to you, because I want you to open first.

But now, I am willing to let you see me, so I may see my innocence.

The gift of Innocence is the gift of seeing everyone through God's eyes. For what is love can only see innocence. And what is love can only create love and its innocence.

What we do cannot take away our innocence—it can only obscure it.

The Verdict:

How do I judge you—innocent.

How did I create you—innocent.

How do I find you—innocent.

How do I see you—innocent.

Why do I love you—you are innocent.

Why do I wish you Home—you are innocent and one with Me.

THE GIFT OF INTEGRITY

When we are at peace with ourselves, we are in touch with the gift of Integrity. Truly, with this gift, we are able to come from the greatest truth.

Often we have tried to be responsible for integrity, and when we have done so, we have found ourselves judging and condemning others. In our management of integrity, we have had to use methods that were themselves, unintegral.

Truly, integrity means coming from the Truth within. Integrity is a gift that we allow to speak through us. Integrity is the presence of our Higher Power. We invite the spirit of Integrity into all our relationships, and all our actions.

The gift of Integrity is the gift of being seen. We allow ourselves and others to see exactly where we are coming from. We allow others to see the depths of our heart. We allow others to connect with us, to share with us, to be with us. It is a gift that hides nothing, nor is its purpose exposure. The gift of Integrity is simply speaking our truth—without excuses, without defence, without denial. We speak of where we are coming from, and we speak of what we would like to see happen.

The gift of Integrity is the ability to honestly ask, and to respect the answers that we are given. With the gift of Integrity, we will always follow our heart.

The gift of Integrity is the gift that speaks of solutions. Truly, the only integral solution is the solution that includes the well-being of everyone. The spirit of Integrity is open to the truth in everyone. With this gift we are always in touch with the truth and the choice within us—we are in touch with what is most healing and loving for all concerned.

Coming from integrity, we come from our connection with all things. It is a realization that we and everything else are an integral part of being. We are connected within and we are connected with those around us. We are each an integral part of each other, of Oneness.

But most importantly, the gift of Integrity connects us with the Wisdom of our Higher Power. His Integrity does not judge—it sees only innocence. His Integrity loves beyond the deepest hatred and darkest fear. His Integrity accepts us where we are and invites us Home. God's Integrity is the truth within us.

We have tried to be integral and have fallen short of this desire many times. We have tried to make the world integral and have become rigid, discouraged and disillusioned. We have forgotten that Integrity is a gift that we may invite in to guide our thoughts, to guide our decisions, to guide our actions. We no longer have to fight for integrity, but we may ask for this gift to come into our lives and the lives of all others. For this gift is the gift of being able to live freely and joyfully with ourselves and with each being in acceptance, and in the spirit of Integrity.

We are not the integrator—the gift of Integrity is.

We do not look after Integrity—we invite the spirit of Integrity to look after us.

THE GIFT OF JOY

The gift of Joy is a gift that has much confusion concerning it. There is much resistance to joy, for at times we are still caught up in our patterns of sadness and despair. We often confuse joy with pleasure and gratification. We sometimes believe that joy is having our goals attained, having our dreams realized. We still believe that joy is a transient thing, quickly replaced by sorrow and anguish.

We have tried to keep out joy because we believed it would soon be followed by loss and depression. We believed, also, in old loyalties to the past—relationships, situations, and any loss that may have occurred in them. To be joyful seemed to negate what had gone on before in our lives. It seemed to deny what had happened.

We have felt sadness, and there has been no room for joy. Joy has seemed elusive, insubstantial, something that could never be attained without much sacrifice, much pain. Most of all, we have not believed that we were entitled to joy. We have not seen that joy was our nature and so much a part of our being as to be inseparable from us.

Let us ask for the gift of Clarity in looking at the Presence of Joy. We have sought joy in many different forms, but we have not understood that this is not where joy is to be found. We have thought joy was a form, an appearance. We were gratified with this focus for a while, but soon the form changed and our seeming joy was lost.

Let us say what joy is:

> *Joy is the **Spirit** of all things.*

It is the Spirit that goes beyond all forms we cling to, beyond all goals we seek, beyond all beliefs we hold. Our forms cannot contain it, for it is that which goes beyond form. Our beliefs cannot maintain it, for it goes beyond all beliefs to the true essence of being.

Joy is what is left when we give up to God all that we think will make us happy. Joy is what is left when we no longer wish to be right. We are sad because so many of our forms have been lost or torn apart. We wish to cling to these forms. We wish to make them, keep them, and maintain them—and in this struggle to honor our forms, we lose sight of joy.

Joy is formless because it is the expression of the God within us. Joy may be expressed through many forms, but it is never the form that is the essence of Joy, it is always the Spirit moving within us and around us.

Our true essence is joy. It cannot be contained; it cannot be squelched; it cannot be buried; it cannot be forgotten. We may lose sight of it in the myriad forms we seek to make us joyful, but joy is eternal and with us always. It is not transient—what is transient are the beliefs and goals we seek to make us happy. What is transient is our seeking apart from God. What is transient is of our making. What is transient is the whole idea that we are alone and separate.

Joy is the Spirit of remembering Who we are. To call on this Spirit is to call on God. As God is Love, so God is Joy.

It seems that if we lose what we have made, we cannot be joyful. But truly, it is what we have made that has kept the knowledge of this Spirit from us. Joy is the essence of all things. It is the well-spring that heals. It is the certainty that remembers Who we are. Always we may answer to the question:

> *"Who am I?"—"I am Joy."*

Yes, there is resistance to joy, for it means acknowledging that the goals we seek will not make us happy. It means acknowledging that what we are right about is our own pain and despair. It means acknowledging that the forms we hold are empty and contain nothing.

The gift of Joy is being in touch with reality of what is eternal, what is important in our lives. The gift of Joy is this reality. The forms we hold on to are illusion. The gift of Joy remembers all that we are, beyond all we have made.

The gift of Joy is the gift of our Being. When we truly acknowledge our being, we are immediately in touch with the gift of Joy—the gift that being with God, that being with the Spirit always brings.

Joy has no conditions—the attaining of what we think will make us happy does. We may ask for joy in the midst of all our forms, in the midst of all our pain, in the midst of all our beliefs. This invitation will take us beyond our sadness, our fear, our desperation.

Joy has seemed to be something we aspire to in spite of all adversity, but we say, joy is the realization that there is no adversity—with God we are connected to the oneness and support of all things.

Joy is seeing what is truly eternal.

It is the recognition of love's presence in the midst of "hatred".

It is the recognition of innocence in the midst of all our judgment and condemnation.

It is the remembrance of asking when we have been walking alone.

> **It is the recognition of solutions where we have seen no way out.**
>
> **It is the recognition of Light where we have seen only darkness.**
>
> **It is the recognition of Self where we have seen only limitations and pettiness.**
>
> **It is the recognition of truth in the midst of our lies, our beliefs.**
>
> **It is the recognition of joy that is our strength, that is our being, and that is our true expression.**
>
> **It is the recognition of God within us, joyfully including all things, and constantly giving all gifts.**

All gifts have Joy at their heart.

THE GIFT OF KNOWING AND SHARING WHO I TRULY AM

We have many strange ideas about who we are. And the strangest of these beliefs is the belief that there is something inherently wrong about our being that can never be corrected. We have thought that any mistakes that we have made, have made us even more wrong, have only proven the wrongness of our being. Some of us have taken suggestions to mean that once again, we were wrong. Circumstances in our lives often seem to confirm the belief that things happen because we are bad, because we are defective, because the very core of our being is wrong.

From this belief come all other strange beliefs that we hold about ourselves. We believe we are undeserving. We believe we cannot be helped—because who would help someone who was so wrong? Who could help someone whose basic being was wrong? We believe we are not enough and will never be enough. We believe that we are weak and ineffectual and we hide this belief in many strange ways and in many strange denials. We hide it in proving our strength, in sickness, in addiction, in conflict and commotion.

We believe our prayers cannot be answered, for who could answer a being so full of sin, so full of wrongs? We believe we cannot be saved, cannot be healed, cannot be helped, cannot be accepted. We hide this belief, but it does not go away. It is the root of our sadness, our desperation, our fears, and our separation from each other and from God.

The gift of knowing and sharing who we truly are takes us out of hiding to see that the thing that is wrong is the entire belief that our being could be wrong, that what God creates could ever be wrong.

The gift of knowing and sharing who we truly are puts us in touch with the "I AM" which is our Source, which is who we truly are. This gift brings back the remembrance of our completeness. This gift lets us recognize the truth and the light within us. It lets us see that our mistakes have nothing to do with our being. It lets us see that when we admit these mistakes, we only become more in touch with the beauty of our being, with the truth of our being.

This gift allows in ideas, suggestions, and another way, because these things do not make us wrong. We may let in everything and choose according to what is for our well-being, to what is for our integrity, and to what accords with the truth within us.

The truth of knowing who we truly are starts with our completeness, starts with us deserving all of God's love and care. From this beginning anything can be corrected and healed. From this beginning anything can come in so the truth within us may clearly see what is real.

Sharing who we truly are is something that we have been afraid to do because we believed that what we truly were was wrong. This was the source of all our hiding. From this source everything we thought, said, or did somehow felt wrong.

With the gift of knowing and sharing who we truly are, we now share our completeness, we now share a being that is totally loved. We now share our mistakes and fears so we may be even more in touch with our true being. We now share our beauty, our wisdom, our innocence. We may let in others with all their ideas, criticisms and suggestions, knowing that none of these affect who we truly are, that none of these make us wrong. With this gift, we may pray to God knowing that we are His child, knowing that our Being, our innocence, our whole-liness is His answer.

Truly, we have only forgotten who we truly are and with this gift comes our Higher Power's remembrance.

THE GIFT OF LAUGHTER

There is an inner laughter which dissolves all fears. It is not a laughter that we pretend or that we use to scorn things. It is not a laughter of affectation or ridicule. It is not a laughter of despair or insanity. It is a laughter that comes from the realization that our fears are not real and our Higher Power will always show us how they may be released. The gift of laughter is the recognition of ourselves. We are reunited with Who we are and the Strength that we are. We are reunited with the Love that we hold and there is a remembrance of our true being.

The gift of laughter is a gift of remembrance. We laugh to remember our lightness of being. We laugh to remember our childlike joy and enthusiasm. We laugh to remember our connection with others.

Laughter is the great healer. It heals all our serious and critical conditions. The gift of laughter recognizes there is nothing so serious that cannot be healed and seen beyond. Yes, laughter is the gift of lightness for we are able to laugh at our own mistakes rather than being riddled with judgment and guilt for having made them.

With the gift of laughter we are able to laugh for the sheer joy of living. We are able to laugh as an expression of our happiness.

With the gift of laughter we are able to laugh with others, knowing they, too, will be healed if they but ask. We may laugh with others in all their struggles and problems, not because their pain is humorous but because we have experienced that pain and know there is another way.

We laugh to remember that we need not stay disconnected from our Source. We laugh to remember there is Light beyond any darkness we see. We know there is connection beyond any separation we feel. We laugh because we cannot stay stuck for too long and we laugh to see ourselves in each other and how we look when we are so serious on being right.

The gift of laughter allows us to look gently on ourselves when we have chosen our way once again.

We laugh to see the ease with which we may let go.

We laugh to see the simplicity with which we may live.

We laugh to see the connectedness beyond all fears of separation.

We laugh at the delightfulness each moment can bring.

The gift of laughter lets us forgive, lets us release and allows us to remember the way Home.

The gift of laughter is the gift of letting go. It is with laughter that we hear the gentle laugh of our Higher Power laughing with us. It is with laughter that we remember all judgment is meaningless. It is with laughter that we are healed and reconnected with our child, with others, and with God.

True laughter is—"There go I."

We laugh from kindness.

We laugh from joy.

We laugh from release and remembrance.

We laugh from seeing ourselves in another.

We laugh in delight of rediscovering ourselves.

We laugh to recognize our own struggles in another.

We laugh to see with what ease these struggles are resolved.

We laugh from opening to Life.

We laugh at our own fears, knowing we will be shown beyond them.

We laugh through our tears that may finally be shed.

We laugh through the darkness that Light is dissolving.

We laugh because we are home and laughter is the very fabric of that home. We laugh because we are happy to be with God once more and Joy is the language that is spoken.

THE GIFT OF LETTING GO

To many of us, letting go has seemed to mean denial. We think we must let go of everything by denying how we feel, what our desires are, what we are holding on to. To let go, we often think we must deny where we are coming from. What occurs in these cases is that we think we have to know how to let go and end up denying ourselves expression and release.

To let go is not to deny, for as long as we deny something, we keep it and obviously we have let go of nothing.

To let go, firstly, let us acknowledge what we are holding on to. Let us be aware of our attachment to whatever we are having difficulty letting go of. It is not to fight to let go. It is not to condemn our holding on. It is not to force ourselves to open our grasp on whatever we are keeping.

The best way to explain letting go is to think of it in terms of letting in. Letting go is truly an opportunity to let in another way. Letting go is an opportunity to ask and receive assistance. Otherwise, letting go becomes a punishment with no possibility of an alternative. Letting go becomes a sacrifice or a denial.

Truly, the gift of letting go is the gift of letting in—letting in solutions, possibilities, choice, and all other gifts that would support and sustain us. We let go in order to have our desperation replaced with Ease. We let go in order to have our attachments to certain goals replaced with the unfoldment of connection and synchronicity.

What we hold on to actually blocks the very thing that we are asking. It narrows and limits our vision. It closes off our awareness to all possible solutions. Anything we hang on to does not allow the natural flow of healing and accomplishment to take place. We let go so that the natural flow may include us in all support, all nurturing, and all well-being.

The gift of letting go, then, includes us in all possible solutions rather than excluding us through our desperation.

Truly, what we are letting go of is our own limited perception of what is best for our well-being, for our happiness, for our safety, for our peace.

We are so afraid to let go because we often believe that it is our holding on that saves us. But, it is to realize that each time we hold on, it is like a closed fist that can receive nothing, that can allow nothing to enter to release the desperation. The flow is blocked. We can neither receive assistance, nor can we express our asking for it. To hold on requires much energy, because we must keep out all of the flow in order to protect what we are holding on to. We literally end up "damning the flow".

It is much easier to consider letting go when we see that choosing our goals, that holding on to our solutions never works, never brings us peace. Truly, the gift of letting go is the point where we realize we are having difficulty opening our fist, but we would like to release what is keeping us prisoner—we would like another way.

Just as it is helpful to think of letting go in terms of letting in, so it is helpful to ask ourselves—what would I like to let go to? If we are holding on to protecting our health, we may ask to let go to the gift of well-being. If we are having difficulty letting go of protecting our safety, we may ask to let go to God's loving care that is all around us. If we are holding on to trying to assure our survival, we may ask to let go to Ease and the support that may come in any form and from any direction.

The gift of letting go is not an act of denial or sacrifice, it is a gift that helps us realize we let in our Higher Power's joy, solutions, nurturing, and wisdom, which is far greater than anything that we have managed to create with our holding on to.

We let go of our day, and are given a day far more joyous and connected than what we could have imagined. We let go of our plans and join in the unfoldment of our deepest desires. We let go of our solutions and come in touch with solutions that include everyone's well-being. We let go of our desperation to survive and are given a life-sense which connects us with all solutions and all possibilities. We let go of our safety and are given love and nourishment. We let go of our dreams and are given vision. We consider letting go of our resentments and are given a joyous sense of freedom and lightness of heart.

We consider letting go of our desperations and are given a new sense of purpose and direction. We consider letting go of our judgments and are given a new depth of understanding and compassion for ourselves and others. We let go of our anger and we are put in touch with an ability to express our true asking. We let go of trying to impress and are given a sharing that comes from the heart. We let go of our lists of things to accomplish and are given the connection with our Higher Power that accomplishes and brings whatever is needed together. We consider letting go of our fears and we experience each and every gift that awaits us.

Letting go is a gift that is present at our request. It is a simple asking for another way. It is a simple knowledge that God's Will for us is far more loving than our protection. It is a simple willingness to let Life in by letting go of our stranglehold on what we think keeps us safe. It is a simple solution that our Higher Power gives when we ask to let go of whatever we have not given to Him to release, dissolve, and to replace with His loving healing.

THE GIFT OF LIFE

Let us breathe the gift of Life. Let us allow Life in, just as we allow a breath of air into our being. There is no judgment in breathing. We allow that Life in without judgment, and we allow that Life to be released without judgment.

So as with breathing, let us allow everything into our lives without judgment, and in this allow the release of letting go. Let us allow the breath of Life with all things.

If there is resistance, allow it to come in without judgment. And, like a breath—allow that resistance to be released without judgment. If there is anger, allow that anger in without judgment. And then, allow it to be released also without judgment. If there is concern, we may breathe it in without judgment and ask for its release—without judgment. Whatever fear is present, we may allow in without having to judge it. We ask for all fears to be breathed out or let go without having to judge them.

We breathe or allow in happiness, but we do not hold on to it—this too is released without judgment. Understand, we let in or breathe in so that our Higher Power may show us that only His loving gifts are real. What we would try to keep out cannot be let in to be released. And what we hold on to, cannot be released to let in even more life and its blessings.

If there is judgment, this too we may allow in without having to judge. And with this entrance, all judgment may be released without us having to judge it.

This is the flow of God's many gifts. We allow everything into our awareness so we may see beyond judgment and so our Higher

Power may release it with our willingness. We breathe life in without having to judge and it is breathed out or released without any need of judgment. This is indeed acceptance. This is the gift of Life.

THE GIFT OF LIGHT

Once upon a time, there was a little candle. This little candle's light shone very pure and bright. This little candle's light was a light that shone from the heart. And the light it gave was very beautiful.

When this little candle came into the world to shine, the candle that received her did not see the brightness and purity of the little candle's heart. This candle was very concerned that the little candle's shape be just so. She was worried that the little candle's wax was not properly formed or just as it should be for the little candle to be a proper candle. This candle fussed over the little candle and in its concern, did not see the light that shone so brightly in the eyes of the little candle.

The big candle began to teach the little candle how a good candle should be. She taught the little candle to worry about the appropriate form and way to shine. And as she did not see the little candle's light, the big candle thought she must give the little candle hers. The big candle could not see the little candle in all its purity and beauty and so it thought it must teach the little candle how to shine and give the little candle its expression.

The little candle could not understand this. She wanted very much to express with her own light and she wondered why the other candle could not see it. Her light felt so pure and true—why could it not be seen?

Then, the little candle began to doubt the light that shone within. And in her doubt, the little candle's radiance grew less and less until it could barely be seen at all. The little candle began to depend upon the big candle to be her light and to give her light. The little candle even began to resent the other candle even while depending on the big candle for her expression.

Soon, the little candle began meeting other candles. They could not see the light within her either. The little candle became more and more sad, for she began to think that any light in her life had to come from the candles around her.

There was something the little candle wanted to express so much, but she did not know what it was. And each time she tried to express this to the other candles, they thought she needed their light and gave her their expression of what they thought a good candle should be.

But inside the little candle there still burned a bright and pure light that wished to shine and radiate to all those around her. The only problem was the little candle no longer trusted this light, for it came from her and she did not see the gift she had to give.

One day, the little candle asked for something that wished to be expressed deep in her heart. She had no words for the asking, only a deep desire for something long ago forgotten, long ago hidden away, long ago unfelt.

And to her asking there came a voice which said:

"Where is the light within you? Why do you not let it shine?"

The little candle became quite desperate and afraid at this request, for she believed there was something wrong with her and she needed all other candles' light so she could shine, so she could express her radiance.

The voice, sensing her concern, gently told her:

> *"Ask for the gift of Light, for the light within you is the gift of your being. No other candle can take it from you, nor can they give it to you, for it is a gift that is present in your very being. This light cannot be lost. You can do nothing wrong to diminish it. You can hide it, but it cannot be extinguished. Ask for the gift of Light and let that gift be your shining. You do not have to hide your light in order to be, for the light* ***is*** *your being. You do not have to prove your light, for truly that is all you are. Do not be resentful at the ones who do not see your light, for they do not see their own. But with the gift of Light, they will see their light reflected in yours.*
>
> *One candle does not have to go out simply because another is shining. Each candle has the same light, and this light comes from within. It comes from the pureness of the heart. Each candle has the same light and in this are all candles connected, are all candles part of the One Light.*
>
> *Ask for your gift and let it come through you. With this gift, you will see all others with the same light. With this gift, all darkness will be shone away. With this gift, all shadows dissolve and melt into nothingness. You may bring anything to this gift and its pureness will light the way for you to follow. Your being is not wrong—it is light. And with this gift, you may ask that the One Light keep the remembrance of light for you. With this gift we light the way for each other by expressing the light within. We light the way for each other by allowing the light of each candle to shine, to radiate, and to express. The light is within. This is your gift."*

And hearing this, the little candle met herself once again. She could see the truth within. She could see her purity. She could see her gift. She could let herself shine and she could let all other candles find their light. She could share her light so all candles could see—the light within.

An enlightened being is one who brings light into the heart.

An enlightened being is one who reflects back the light within us.

An enlightened being is one who encourages us to let our light shine.

An enlightened being is one who sees our light.

THE GIFT OF LOVE

There is much talk about what direction to take. There is much thought about which path to follow. There is much deliberation about which decision to make. There is much concern about doing the right thing. What is our purpose? Is this purpose going in the right direction? Are we doing what we are supposed to be doing? And if not, what is our direction to be?

In answer to all these questions, we may ask ourselves one thing—what is truly important in our lives? Looking at this question, we find that the only thing that has had any meaning to us, any importance, has been those times when we were able to give or receive love—when we recognized love's presence, when we were in the presence, the all-encompassing presence, of love.

Truly, all of our questions of meaning, purpose, and direction can be answered with the gift of Love. It sounds so incredibly simple, yet, is it not love that we seek? When we find ourselves empty, is it not the awareness of love that we lack? Is not all our search to find glimpses of this great Power?

Yes, we try to control love. We try to make it. We try to bind it. We forget that it is a gift from God and, in truth, is God. How many times have we heard, "God is Love"? Is this not our direction—"Sought through prayer and meditation to increase our conscious contact with God..."—sought through prayer and meditation to increase our conscious contact with Love.

It seems that this sort of direction is very intangible, yet truly, after all our plans, all our decisions, all our management, the only thing that truly has any meaning for us is the love we have felt-- the pure, unconditional love we felt in certain moments of our lives.

The gift of Love is the meaning with which we live. Are we asking with Love? Are we answering with Love? Do our words, our actions come from Love?

The gift of God's Love is the direction we seek. Does our direction come from Love and does our direction seek more ever to open to this Love?

The gift of Love is our healing. It is our grace of forgiveness. The gift of Love is our strength and our safety, for there is nothing stronger than this gift.

The gift of Love is our Light. And there is no light more pure or radiant.

The gift of Love is our prayer in which we find the meaning and the purpose of life.

The gift of Love is that fulfillment of the God within us, of the God which is expressed all around us.

The gift of Love is what we have to say, what we have to do. It is all meaning; it is all direction; it is all purpose.

The gift of Love is our very being, and it is this gift that is our direction, that is our power, and that is our purpose.

The gift of Love is all there is.

Love is the direction.

Love is the purpose.

Love is the meaning.

Love is the gift.

Love is our being.

Love is.

THE GIFT OF MEANING

It is when we feel most disconnected with life that we search for its meaning. It is when we feel lost and separate that life has no meaning for us. It is when we are trying to figure out the meaning of life that it loses its meaning and becomes something very serious and seemingly outside of ourselves.

If we were to ask: "When does life have the most meaning for you?" it would soon be recognized that life has the most meaning when we are connected—connected with the moment, connected with ourselves, connected with each other, and connected with our Higher Power. It is in these moments of connection that we find the gift of meaning.

We find that it is not what we have made that ultimately has meaning for us. Meaning is to be found in each gift that God would give us. When we are connected with our Source, the question of meaning does not even arise.

When we are allowing Life to live through us, we are at the center of meaning. When we are allowing Love to flow through us, we are at the center of meaning.

Meaning is the Spirit of all things. If we put form first, we will lose the sense of meaning, for what has meaning is the Spirit that flows through and makes use of the form.

The gift of Meaning is to be found in the moment, for that is where there is all connection. The gift of Meaning is to be found when we share who we are and when we allow others to express their being. The gift of Meaning is to be found when we reach out, and when we open to each other.

We cannot find the gift of Meaning alone, for the gift of Meaning is the gift of Inclusion. The gift of Meaning brings us together to share our uniqueness and to share our gifts. There is meaning when we see:

> *"There by the grace of God go I."*

The gift of Meaning is also to be found in simplicity, for truth is simple, and what is truthful has all of love's meaning.

By ourselves, there is no meaning simply because we are not by ourselves. To have the gift of Meaning we must have the gift of each other, we must have that connection of love and recognition. And what gives meaning to anything is being connected with our Higher Power, from Whom the gift of all meaning flows.

In each gift is all meaning. The gift of Meaning is truly to be in the gift of Life. The gift of Meaning is to be found in letting go, so that all meaning can be given. "Thy meaning, not my meaning, be done."

When I share who I am, I share the gift of Meaning.

When I listen to who you are, I share the gift of Meaning.

When I let go of my fears and ask for another way, I share the gift of Meaning.

When I let you see my pain, I share the gift of Meaning.

When I let you see my joy, I share all that is meaningful.

When I see you and I are one, I am living the gift of Meaning.

When I let my Higher Power guide me, I am given all Meaning.

THE GIFT OF MIRACLES

When we have lived a life run on self-will and desperation, it is indeed a miracle to consider the possibility of God's gifts.

The gift of Miracles shows us the tremendous wonder in letting go of our management of life in order to truly receive the gift of Life.

The gift of Miracles is a gift of God's solutions. When we ask for our Higher Power's assistance, we experience the miracle of having an impossible problem resolved. We experience the love that the miracle always brings. The miracle is that there is always a solution and that solution always has its basis in God's love, in God's healing.

The gift of Miracles is experienced when we let go and invite in another way—our Higher Power's way.

The gift of Miracles is a bridge that brings God's gifts to us. It is a miracle because it is not limited by our controls, our conclusions, and our beliefs. It is a miracle because it includes all the possibilities of a loving solution that is for everyone's well-being.

In asking for the gift of Miracles, we experience the healing power that is found in a moment. We experience the wonder of our relationships being replaced with what is honest, true and supportive. We see the miracle of God's care for us. We feel the miracle of being at peace with ourselves and others. We feel the miracle of acceptance. We experience the miracle of healing and reconnection. We see the miracle of broken relationships being healed and released. We see the miracle of innocence. We find the miracle of faith and trust. We come to know the miracle of our inner child experiencing life and joy. We participate in the miracle of oneness and light. We feel the miracle of being with our Higher Power and allowing Him to guide and care for us.

The gift of Miracles is the gift that says:

> *"Here are God's gifts, please accept them—they will work miracles."*

The gift of Miracles is the gift that takes us beyond all that we have been using, all we have been controlling, all we have been fighting, and shows us there is another way.

A miracle is not of our doing, but it includes us in the very heart of all being and all expression.

The gift of Miracles is the gift of being given ourselves—truly healed, complete, innocent and whole.

The gift of Miracles is the gift of remembrance, remembrance of what is already ours, of what has never been lost, and of what has been constantly given.

God is the miracle. Love is the miracle. Each of us is the miracle.

The gift of Miracles is the gift of reconnection. We are reconnected with all that we are and all that we have to give. We are reconnected with the gifts. We are reconnected with God. We are reconnected with Life, and all its miracles.

Miracles are not the manifestation of our solutions. If we are asking for the gift of Miracles, we are truly asking that our solutions be replaced with God's healing solutions. It is a miracle because it is not our solution—it is a Higher solution, based on Self-will.

A miracle is not proof of love, for love cannot be proven. A miracle is simply an expression of love that we experience each time we are willing to ask for the gift of Miracles to heal each relationship and circumstance.

Prayer:

Show me the miracle of Your Love in this situation, because I only see resentment and hatred.

Show me the miracle of Your healing, because I cannot stop seeing what is dis-eased.

Please give me the miracle of Your release, because I am too afraid to let go.

Please bring me the miracle of Your faith, because I am overwhelmed by doubt and confusion.

Please show me the light of Your care, because I feel alone and lost in darkness.

Please show me the miracle of my innocence, because I cannot accept myself or see Who I am.

Please bring me the miracle of Your vision, for I see myself and others with eyes of judgment, guilt and condemnation.

Please show me the miracle of life, because I have been fighting life and do not trust it.

Please be the miracle in my life.

--Amen

THE GIFT OF MOTIVATION

Often we have tried to motivate ourselves and others. We have thought that we must come up with motivation for special projects, for certain actions, for certain jobs, and for specific directions. We have sought to come up with motivation for ourselves and we have sought to inspire motivation in others, and have found this very tiring indeed. We knew we lacked motivation in our lives, but somehow we weren't quite sure how to be motivated or if we were motivated, we weren't sure how to maintain this pace.

Often what we found ourselves motivated by was guilt and even fear. If we didn't do something that we thought we should be doing, we used the motivation of guilt to begin accomplishing what we thought was necessary. We used pressure, deadlines, tension, to motivate ourselves into action, and ultimately as a final trump card, our life was motivated by fear. We feared the worst happening if we didn't do something. We feared chaos if we didn't control situations, and this fear became a motivator.

We thought fear motivated us to be safe. We thought fear motivated us to be caring and responsible. We thought fear motivated us to do what was right and to be the best we could be—but still, in spite of all this "motivation" we felt less and less motivated in our lives.

Let us look at the Gift of Motivation. With this gift we are not required to motivate ourselves. It is a gift given to us. The gift of our Higher Power's Motivation is somewhat different than the motivation we have been trying to manufacture. This gift begins, not with guilt, but with our innocence. Can you imagine being motivated by innocence? God's Gift of Motivation begins with our completeness and is a motivation of Peace. Can you imagine being motivated by a sense of your Higher Power's Love for you?

We are no longer motivated by "have-to's".

With the gift of Motivation, we are motivated by "choose-to's", by willingness, by enthusiasm, and by consideration.

The gift of Motivation supplies us with the very enthusiasm for Life and for the expression of the Love within us that motivation is truly about.

We are no longer self-motivated, but God or Higher-Self motivated. Our motivation has a different Source now. We are motivated with Love—not fear. We are motivated with Inspiration—not desperation. We are motivated with Enthusiasm—not despair. We are given motivation by our Higher Power, and Love is our Higher Power's motivator.

THE GIFT OF MY INNER CHILD

Deep within a child still waits—judged,
condemned and bound.
Deep within a child still waits—hoping to
be found.

Deep within a child still holds—the fears
we've called his sins.
But deep inside a child still holds—all the
gifts he's ever been.

Deep within a child still waits—afraid of dark
and night.
But deep within a child we find—a pure and
radiant light.

Deep within we find ourselves and here
forgiveness lies.
For deep within we find ourselves seen
through a small child's eyes.

Somewhere, we have become disconnected from our being. Somewhere, a little child within us began to see itself as wrong or bad. Somewhere, many years ago, the child mistakenly interpreted any lack of love towards it as meaning there was something lacking in itself, in its being. Somewhere, words were mistakenly interpreted to mean that the child was defective in some way. Somewhere, at birth, after birth, or even in the countless time before birth, there was an idea that there was something very inherently wrong in the soul, in the core of this being.

Words were spoken to the child that were not loving. Actions perhaps showed the child that it was not always wanted. Other beings, with a sense of disconnection from their own child, often taught the child their own fears and disconnections. They passed on the belief—"There is something wrong with us."

Often we were taught to "Grow up!" There was a hope that if we grew up very, very fast, then we would not have to feel that sense of wrongness, that separation again. The adults in our lives did not always wish to be reminded of their own vulnerable, lost child. They wished us to grow up so they would not have to feel that part of themselves that had always felt "wrong".

Somewhere along the way, our child received the impression that it was not okay to express itself, to feel, or to be. It got the impression that it had to pretend to be something else—it had to pretend to be grown-up, mature, responsible.

A lot of us have not wanted to be in touch with our inner child, for to do so would bring back old feelings of helplessness, of being unlovable, of feeling out of place, of feeling wrong.

And so there are many of us adults walking around trying to be grown up, and still feeling disconnected, confused, and lost. There is part of us missing. There is a part of us still cut off, suppressed, blamed, and condemned. We have left our child locked inside and have accepted all judgments and limiting conclusions about it.

We have accepted many of the things our parents and other adults have said about us. We have accepted that we were lazy, stupid, embarrassing, too noisy, disruptive, a nuisance. We have accepted that we were not beautiful, coordinated, gifted, valuable. We have accepted that we would not amount to much, that we did not try hard enough, that we did not do enough, that we weren't smart enough, brave enough, good enough, and all the many things that in their own rage and frustration, our parents, relatives, teachers, friends dumped upon us. We have accepted others' perceptions of ourselves and we have been running from that child ever since, trying to put as much distance between ourselves and that child as possible. We have abandoned this child, locking it deep within us.

The only problem is—we are that child and that child is still looking for love outside itself. We have not seen that true love for ourselves comes from an acceptance of what is within.

The gift of our inner child is the gift of finally being connected again with the child we disowned; with the part of us we condemned so many years ago. It is the gift of love and connection with our entire being. It is a gift that shows us that truly we are none of those judgments placed upon us. We are simply a child calling for love in the only way we know how.

The gift of our inner child is the gift that shows us beyond all the judgments, ever made about us and says: "Here is your child, how beautiful, loving, and wise it is. Look how much love it has to give. Look how much happiness and joy it has inside of it. Look how sad it has been since you rejected it and saw its being as wrong. Look how easily it forgives and wants to join with you again. Look how much it has to share and offer. Look how simply it trusts when you reach out your hand in honesty to it. Look how bright and shining are its eyes beyond its tears and fears of rejection and abandonment."

You do not have to abandon your child any longer. It is a very wise being who can show you how it is to be loved and what it truly wishes for your entire well-being.

The gift of our inner child is a gift of being at one with ourselves again. It is accepting that part that we thought was wrong, only to find its innocence once more. We find our child is okay—it simply wants to be loved and accepted. We find our child is not wrong or bad—it has simply been afraid.

The gift of our inner child has even one further gift. For in finding our own inner child, we find the child in each other—the child that wishes to be loved. The child that feels out of place and that it does not belong. The child that is innocent. In other words—we find each other again. "...and a child shall lead them."

The kingdom of heaven is with our child, for truly that is all we are—children of God. And the greatest maturity that anyone can have is the heart of a child.

We are truly gifted with our inner child, and meeting and accepting the gift of our inner child is truly the greatest gift of all.

THE GIFT OF NEVER HAVING TO WALK ALONE

Truly, opening to all the gifts means never having to walk alone. With each gift is the Presence of our Higher Power. With each gift we are given what is needed for our care and well-being. With each gift we are given guidance and direction. All our gifts are given to us by One Who walks with us every step of the way.

How can we be alone when there is the gift of inner knowing? How can we be alone when we have the gift of supportive friends? How can we be alone when we see the gift of what we have to give? How can we be alone with the gift of being seen and heard?

Each time we are willing to ask, we are in the Presence. Each time we are willing to invite another way, our journey is accompanied by all of Heaven.

We only are alone when we have decided that we must manage the doing. We are alone in our rightness and in each judgment we choose to make. We are alone when we feel resentment, when we are not in touch with the true gift that we are.

And even in this we are not alone. There is One Who walks beside us with an outstretched hand, inviting us Home. The gifts but await our asking. They do not disappear. We do not forfeit them. They simply wait on invitation. No, even in our feeling alone, we are not alone. The help, the solutions, the caring is but a moment away.

The gift of never having to walk alone is truly a wonderous gift when it is realized, not only Who walks beside us, but with Whose Strength our walking is done—Whose Strength is within us. We are not alone in our journey, for with this gift, we will see we were never alone. We will see in each person another soul willing to have gentle company on their journey. We will see the deep yearning in all of us to reconnect with something that is not larger than ourselves, but is ourselves.

The gift of never having to walk alone is the gift that heals all fears. There is no dark tunnel. There is no valley of the shadow of death. For with this gift, all thoughts of death dissolve in the light of the One Who accompanies us. The Light is with us each step of the way so that all our terrors may be seen beyond.

The gift of never having to walk alone is the gift of meeting the strength inside of us. It is the gift of seeing the Power of the Love that we are.

The gift of never having to walk alone brings us in touch with all we were ever connected to. We, who have felt so alone, need keep this illusion no longer.

The gift of never having to walk alone is the gift of reconnection and remembrance. We remember Who we are and we remember we are one with the Source Who has never left us.

THE GIFT OF NURTURING

It is no accident that "nature" and "nurture" are so close in their sound and meaning. It is difficult for some of us to see God as nurturing, for we have been taught to perceive God as a stern father image. The idea that God is nurturing seems foreign, for our perception of God has been incomplete and has not included that aspect which is mothering, which is nurturing.

To be nurtured is to be cared for. It is to be looked after, supported and encouraged to be all that we can be. To be nurtured is to be surrounded by gentleness and affection. It is to be enfolded in arms of great caring, great love, and great freedom.

The gift of nurturing continually replenishes and restores; it is an endless well of comfort. When we are nurtured, we are given new strength, and from this core of care we may open as a flower to the light.

The gift of nurturing shows us a God that is our father and our mother, for the Source must be the Source of All Things.

The gift of nurturing lets us allow God to care for us. It is the mothering our child has always desired.

We need to come back to God in all God's aspects. The God of our understanding has been incomplete, vengeful and, in many cases, vindictive. Some of us have been taught of a God that punishes if we do not follow His Will. The God of our understanding has often been fearful.

The gift of nurturing, the gift of nurture, puts us in touch with the God that wishes only to enfold us in "Her" gentle care. The gift of nurturing gives us that nourishment with which we can nurture others, for it is a gift we all possess.

The gift of nurturing is a continual renewal of Life and it is that Life within us that our Higher Power nurtures.

It is time to let God enfold us and hold us close, in order that our being can flower and go beyond all limits. It is our nature to be nourished, to be nurtured, and it is our nature to nourish—to nurture.

We have gone a long way from the energy of nurture. We have not nurtured each other, our homes, or all other things with which we live.

The gift of nurturing is a new beginning, for with its acceptance may we know the healing power of being nurtured once again. And with this gift may we pass on all the healing that our acceptance of this gift has brought. May we be nurtured in God and be reconnected once more with God as the Source of all nurturing.

THE GIFT OF OPENING

The gift of Opening allows us to receive. Ultimately, what we open to is our Higher Power guiding our hearts and filling our lives with His gifts.

The gift of Opening opens us to ourselves. We have judged many things about ourselves and have not been prepared to open to let anyone see what we hide within. We have been afraid to open because when we open, everything that we have hidden becomes visible. And so, we have remained closed, refusing gifts because we were afraid of what others would see when we opened.

We believed that opening opened us to criticism and condemnation. We believed that opening opened us to further pain and manipulation. We believed that opening opened us to people who would take advantage of us, who would hurt us. We believed that opening opened us to loss, to people leaving when they saw who we really were. We believed that opening only opened us to others' controls, to others' ridicule, and to others' ultimate rejection. We have not seen opening as a gift at all but rather something to avoid at all costs.

And so, we have held back. We have held back opening to each other. We have held back expression and creativity. We have held back asking and answering. We have held back being fully present. We have held back support, love, affection. We have held back tears, laughter, anger, and all other feelings. We have held back our knowing. We have held back our beauty. We have held back our giving. But most of all, we have held back receiving any of our Higher Power's gifts. Our lives have become one big holdback because we are afraid to open.

The gift of opening shows us what it is we are truly opening to. When we finally open to the gift of Opening, we no longer have to hide what has kept us fearful and dis-eased. When we open to let others see us, we open to healing. With the gift of Opening, our Higher Power is the opening through which we receive all gifts. With our Higher Power, we are able to open to love. With our Higher Power, we are able to open to choices that are always appropriate for us. With our Higher Power, we open to solutions, rather than close from fear.

The gift of Opening allows us to fully receive all other gifts. We open to gifts, not to judgments. It is in our opening that all judgments will be seen beyond. We open to acceptance, not condemnation, for with the gift of Opening, all that has been condemned will be able to be seen another way.

We open to our Higher Power being in charge of our lives. And with this gift, what we open to will always be appropriate, will always be healing, and will always be a gift.

Open to Me and I will be your opening.

Open to Me and let Me open you to the choice for well-being.

Open to Me and let Me open your eyes to true vision and light.

Open to Me and let Me open your awareness to all the gifts that are yours.

Open to Me and let Me open your day.

Open to Me and let Me open you to life and all its expression opening within you.

In our admittance of who we are, we will open to ourselves.

In our admittance of our mistakes, we will open to another way.

In our admittance of our fears, we will open to the light.

In our admittance of what we try to control, we will open to release.

In our admittance to each other, we will open to connection.

In our admittance of our powerlessness, we will open to One Who has All Power.

In our admittance of weakness, we will open to strength.

In our admittance of our addiction, we will open to freedom.

In our admittance that we cannot do it alone, we will open to a Power greater than ourselves, a Power within ourselves, that will open us to all gifts and all opening.

THE GIFT OF OUR HIGHER POWER'S GIFTS EACH DAY

We usually think we know what would make us happy. We think that if only we could achieve certain goals, our life indeed would be joyous. Often we pray to God in order to have Him fulfill those aims and objectives that we think will bring happiness to us.

We have very definite ideas about what would make us happy and what would keep us happy. We have definite ideas about what would bring us joy. We think we know what would bring love into our lives. We think we know what love should look like and what would bring love to us. We have definite ideas about what support should look like. We ask for all these gifts to come in very specific ways, predetermined by us. We still think we know how these gifts should come to us.

The gift of our Higher Power's gifts for us is indeed a treasure. Instead of asking God for joy, our way, we now ask for the gift of God's Joy, His Way—"Please give me Your Joy today." We are finally ready to accept the gifts our Higher Power would give us rather than our own limited goals of what would make us happy. The gifts our Higher Power would give us are far beyond our experience and our own desperate attempts to find happiness our way. The gift of our Higher Power's gifts each day goes far beyond what we desperately search for, to the true essence of all gifts.

Our Higher Power's gifts are unconditional and with this gift comes the miracle and wonder of each new day. This is the gift of freedom, for we are relying on God's Will for us and the miraculous gifts that this would bring.

THE GIFT OF PEACE

What would one not give for peace of mind? What would one not give to awaken to a peace of mind that was not threatened, shaken, or disturbed in any way? What would one not give to find peace in any situation? What would one not give to find peace with one's self and with one's family? What would one not give to have a sense of peace that went beyond all anger and resentment—a sense of peace that went beyond all conclusions, all circumstances, and all beliefs? What would the world not give for peace, for the harmony that comes when peace is chosen?

The gift of Peace is the gift of being able to live with one's Self. We have been at war with ourselves, carrying many shoulds, judgments, and embittered conclusions. With this gift, we are at peace with our hearts, we are at peace in our mind, we are at peace in our spirit.

The gift of Peace does not require that we accept what has happened to us; it asks us to let go of what we think happened to us in order to begin life anew.

The gift of Peace is the acceptance of our true worth and holiness. We are at peace with our oneness and with our connection to all things. We have peace with our brothers when we see our own holiness reflected in their eyes.

The gift of Peace is the gift of seeing our true value. It is the gift of being with the Holy Source whose child we are. The gift of Peace is seeing our wholeness and completeness, for if we were to truly see our strength and our completeness, there would be no envy, there would be no resentment, there would be no insecurity, there would be no conflict.

The gift of Peace offers us connection with the truth of who we are. It is the gift of completeness and wholeness. It is the gift of inner strength and wisdom. It is the gift that passes understanding—our understanding—to the understanding of who we are and the gifts that each of us has to offer.

Peace of mind is the awareness that we are whole—wholly loving, wholly giving, wholly worthy, and wholly cared for.

The gift of Peace takes us beyond all beliefs in lack and separation. It teaches us we lack nothing, nor are we separate from anything.

The gift of Peace is not the absence of conflict—the gift of Peace is the presence of Love; it is the presence of Healing; it is the presence of solutions; it is the presence of caring and understanding; it is the presence of a Power greater than our little egos, yet including all of us.

No, peace is not an absence from; it is inviting in the Presence of our Higher Power, our Higher Self.

There is nothing that the Peace of God cannot heal. There is no illusion that the Peace of God cannot dissolve. There is no doubt, there is no question that the Peace of God cannot answer. There is no conflict or difficulty that the gift of Peace cannot resolve.

What would one not give for a gift such as this—the gift that allows us to truly live with ourselves and with each other in total love and harmony? For if we have the gift of Peace, we have everything. We've gone beyond anger, fear, pain, and any other illusion that would hold us in each and every situation.

What would we give for peace?—everything. And what we are given in return are all the gifts, all the peace that our Higher Power has to offer.

One gift is not dependent on another. Our peace is not dependent on being happy, nor is happiness dependent on being at peace. All gifts occur simultaneously. You cannot have one gift without receiving all gifts. We do not have to earn peace. We do not have to prepare for peace. We do not have to maintain peace, nor uphold it. We cannot make the peace. We cannot manufacture it. All our attempts to make peace have resulted in conflict. We are not peacemakers, but with willingness we may ask to receive this gift and in our receiving we will have this gift to give.

We have forgotten the Source from which all peace comes and when we forget this, we forget Who we are and find ourselves in conflict once again.

Anytime we forget that something is a gift, we will assume responsibility for it. And in this assumption, we will try to protect and we will lose the very thing we seek. It is to remember that it is not our peace that will heal anything. We are speaking of the Peace of God Who upholds and maintains this gift for everyone. No sacrifice, no duties, no requirements are needed—only a simple asking is all that is required for this gift to be given. There is nothing to learn, there is no pain to undergo in order to ask for this gift. There is nothing to be paid. When we receive this gift, we will not wish our old ways, our old conclusions, and our old fears. There is nothing to lose, only all heaven to gain.

This gift is truly our heart's desire, and we will recognize this gift because it is already ours and because it is already within us.

May God's Peace be with you.

May you remember It always.

The Peace of God is truly the center of all things. To be at Peace is not an absence of activity, but the very center of all expression, creativity and solutions. With this gift we are in touch with our full capacities and our ability to share these gifts.

The gift of Peace is the center of all awareness, all understanding, all knowledge. It is the very heart of Life. It is the very heart of our Being. It is the very heart of God.

Each time I give everything in order to have Peace—I am given everything.

THE GIFT OF PRACTICING THE PRESENTS OF GOD

Quite often our priorities are not concerned with putting our Higher Power first. Our priorities are such that we wish to accomplish them first and then we think we will turn to our Higher Power for peace and healing. Placing our Higher Power first is something we continually forget to do, and consequently, we continually find ourselves in conflict and in struggle.

In order to receive God's gifts, we need to recognize that God is the gift from which all gifts come. In placing our Higher Power first, we also place well-being, happiness, connectedness, support, care, and all other gifts first. Practicing the presents of God is simply choosing God first above all our goals, all our accomplishments, all our desperations. In practicing the presents of God, it is truly our Higher Power that does the doing. With this gift, we do not have to know how to be with God—it is given. We do not need to know how to practice these presents, we need only ask to have the presents to be with us all the time.

Practicing the presents is simply being with the Presence. It is simply a choice—"Do I wish my way, with my goals, or do I wish my Higher Power's Presence with all His gifts?"

When we practice the presents of God, all his gifts are expressed. Thus we practice Love, Trust, Compassion, Understanding, Caring, Forgiveness, and all other gifts that are given.

We can only practice what we are given, what we are willing to receive. We can only practice the presents if we are willing to receive God's presents.

The very admittance: "I don't know how," and a willingness to ask for God's presents is the practicing. We don't have to get it right, we don't have to know how to do it, we don't need to know how to maintain the practicing—we need only ask for the Presence to enter.

Practicing the presents of God is a willingness to put God first, second, third, and eternally in our lives. This is a gift, also, which will be given the moment we ask for it, the moment we admit—"I can't manage stopping my goals, please give me Your presents instead."

With the gift of practicing the presents of God, the practice is perfect. Really, practicing the Presence of God is expressing the will of God and, with this gift, it is He Who does the expressing, the putting of this Will into practice.

THE GIFT OF RECOGNIZING GIFTS

Each day we are given all gifts. Each day we fail to recognize this. We still see judgment instead of acceptance. We still see condemnation instead of appreciation. The gifts are all around us, but we do not always see this.

There is a gift of recognition that all may ask for—the gift of recognizing gifts.

In each situation there is a gift that we may ask to see. In each person there is a gift offered to us. In ourselves there is a gift waiting to be expressed and given. We are in a sea of gifts. And with this particular gift, we will be able to see this.

By ourselves we have been unable to recognize our gifts. The gift of recognizing gifts comes from our Higher Power. It is with His recognition that each gift is seen. It is with His awareness that gifts may be appreciated. It is with His gratitude that gifts may be received.

The true recognition is that our Higher Power is the real Gift in everything. It is not that our Higher Power bestows these gifts upon us—they are already given; they are already ours. Our Higher Power will only show us what is ours already, what is always given to us.

It is not with ***our*** recognition that we will recognize our gifts—it is with the gift of recognition.

Prayer:

In each circumstance I find myself in today, there will be a gift—please show it to me, please be my recognition.

I do not know the gifts I hold, please help me recognize the gifts that are already in my heart so I may express them.

In each person I will meet today, there is a gift—please help me see it, please be my recognition.

Please show me the gift of asking You, so I may recognize all other gifts.

Please help me recognize these gifts are mine, given lovingly by You.

Please help me recognize the beauty, the trust, the faith, the support, the love, the caring, and all other gifts I have forgotten and did not recognize.

Please help me recognize the Gift of You in all gifts.

--Amen

THE GIFT OF RELEASE (REAL EASE)

We have held on to many things thinking they were important. We have held on to old ideas that we thought would save us. We have held on to old resentments to remind ourselves not to let these situations occur again. We have held on to old beliefs and defended them with our lives. We have held on to old memories that we thought proved our expertise and worth. We have held on to people, places and things. We have held on to old dreams of how things should have been. We have held on to guilt and remorse. We have held on to grief and sadness. We have held on to all the things we have "lost" and have wished desperately to have them back again.

We have held on to working and learning with struggle and conflict, believing that that was the only way God would reward us. We have held on to ideas of sacrifice, to ideas of management, and to ideas of control. We have held on to anger and revenge. We have held on to our judgments. We have held on to pushing to get our way. We have held on to sickness for the uses we thought it brought to us. We have held on to being right. We have held on to how things should be. We have held on to who has "wronged" us and we have held on to the shame of those we have "wronged". We have held on to what we thought would protect us and we have become overwhelmed with this burden of protection. We have even held on to our beliefs in God and how God should be worshipped.

We have held on to relationships, too afraid to turn them over to our Higher Power. We have held on to our work, thinking it would make us worthy. We have held on to certain relationships, thinking they would make us loved. We have held on to our expertise and learning, thinking that would bring us recognition. We have held on to the image we have created, thinking that's what people wanted to see. We have held on to "truth", thinking our truth would set us free. We have held on to everything and released very little.

It is time for the gift of Release. It is time to let go of our collection of pain, resentment, beliefs, ideas, relationships, expertise, and "truth".

The gift of Release releases us from all that we hold and replaces it with God's Ease. God is Ease—Real Ease. God is release of all judgments and condemnation.

The gift of Real Ease shows us the Ease with which we may be. It is the gift which shows us the Ease in each situation by showing us what we may release to our Higher Power's care.

We release everything to the care of our Higher Power and are given the gift of Real Ease.

Ease is the gift with which we may release all that we hold. Before, it has been like taking in a breath and never releasing it. Now, we are given the breath of release. We have held many things, but have not released them into our Higher Power's Ease. Our life has not been easy, for what we hold, what we do not release, blocks the gift of God's Ease.

The gift of Release is the gift of letting go all that we have held on to. We make room for Life. We release in order to let in, in order to let well-being, love, joy, respect, understanding, forgiveness enter. What we hold on to blocks each of God's gifts from entering our lives. For each thing we let go of, we are given the gift of Release so our lives may be lived with Real Ease.

We are released from pain. We are released from resentment. We are released from judgments and ideas that have never served us. We are released from prejudice. We are released from struggle and conflict. We are given the gift of release so we may let go of all that has kept us stuck and imprisoned. We are able to live with Real Ease.

Prayer:

Please release whatever I am holding and replace it with Your Ease.

Please show me that Ease does it.

Please release me from the fears I hold and give me Your Ease in living.

Please release me from my resentments and replace them with Your Ease in forgiving.

Please take all my reminders to hold on and replace them with Your healing reminders to let go to Your Ease.

Please take all the tensions with which I remember all my resentments, all my ideas, all my worth, and replace them with Your Healing Ease, with Your Breath of Life.

Please release my management and replace it with the Ease of Your Solutions.

Please release my collection and replace it with all Your gifts that hold me in Your Care.

--Amen

THE GIFT OF REMEMBERING TO ASK FOR ALL GIFTS

Many times during the day we get caught up in what appears to be happening around us. We get caught up in commotions. We get caught up in struggle and confusion. We get caught up in arguments, in wanting to be right. We get caught up in trying to do it ourselves without the assistance of a Higher Power. We get caught up in endless lists of shoulds and have-to's. We get caught up in fixing people and trying to help them our way. We get caught up in helplessness, hopelessness, and discouragement. We get caught up in all the old ways and all the old thinking. We get caught up and we forget to ask.

The gift of remembering to ask is a tiny bit of sanity that we allow to come into the insanity we find ourselves involved in. This tiny remembrance is the gift that brings a mighty light to shine away all the shadows we are seeing. And what we remember to ask for is God's gifts—the gifts that are present beyond the meaningless insanity of what seems to be happening to us.

The gift of Remembrance is a gift that reminds us that we are back into our way rather than into our Higher Power's way. It is the gift that reminds us to ask—we may ask for our Higher Power's solution, our Higher Power's patience, our Higher Power's understanding, our Higher Power's forgiveness, in each situation where we find conflict and frustration.

This gift is a remembrance to ask. It is a gift that reminds us—have you asked for God's Gifts today, have you asked for God's Gifts with this person or in that situation?

The gift of Remembrance is the gift of Light in a dark world. We can remember to ask for light. We don't have to try to remember, for sometimes we are too caught up in our insanities to remember there is another way. We don't have to try to remember to ask for God's Gifts, for this too is a gift. God's Remembrance is a reminder to ask for His Gifts. Even remembrance is given so we may always ask to come Home no matter how far we have traveled, no matter how far we have become lost in the darkness.

Remembrance is kept for us, asking is kept for us, and all our gifts are kept for us. Our Higher Power will be our remembering, our rejoining.

Re-member is to become one with again—to rejoin. Dis-member is to forget the Source of all our gifts and in this we feel separate and alone.

Remembrance is a gift.

THE GIFT OF RESPECT

The gift of Respect allows being. We are given respect for our being and the being of others. The gift of respect recognizes the wisdom, the connectedness and the light in everyone.

The gift of respect sees past the illusions we try to make real in order to see the true reality, the true divinity of another being.

The gift of Respect is the gift of allowing. We are given the gift of allowing ourselves to be. We respect the feelings we need to feel, the words we need to say, and the sharing we need to share. We respect the healing that needs to take place, the asking we need to get in touch with. We are respectful of our beginning—our beginning to be well, whole and complete. We are respectful of our being a beginner, of not knowing. We are respectful of our mistakes—not in order to condone them, but so we may be respectful that we may make them, and in this respect, ask for them to be corrected.

We are given the gift of Respect beyond our fears. We are given the gift of respect beyond our impatience and wanting to fix. We are given respect in the midst of our fixing and being fixed. And truly, the gift of Respect is—it is okay to **be**. The gift of Respect says: "I know you, too, will find healing." The gift of Respect says:

> *"No matter what I see, there is that within you, within me, that is complete."*

The gift of Respect is truly being able to see ourselves with eyes of forgiveness, with eyes of compassion and gentleness. The gift of Respect is being able to see ourselves in each other—"By the Grace of God, there go I."

The gift of Respect connects us with all living things, for truly all living things are worthy of respect, of acknowledgment. Respect is the great connector, the great opener that allows in love, caring, trust, and innocence.

We are given our Higher Power's Respect which allows us to find ourselves in the midst of whatever we are feeling or doing. We are given the respect of being able to be. We gift others with the gift of being able to be. We do not fix, but even if this should occur, there is still the gift of Respect which says:

> *"Let us choose again. Let us even go beyond this separation so we may see completeness in each other."*

We salute our being and we salute the being of others.

There is no need to prove our being, to defend it, to hide it, to try to be it—it is a gift given with our Higher Power's Respect.

Prayer:

Please give me Your Respect so I may let others be, and in this see the freedom of my own being.

Please give me Your Respect so I may treat myself with dignity wherever I may happen to be, whatever I may happen to be doing.

Please give me Your Respect so I may see and acknowledge the gift of all beings.

Please give me Your Respect so I may truly hear and see my brother.

Please give me Your Respect so I may see my freedom to be well.

Please give me Your Respect so I may be with all respect—loving and caring.

Please give me Your Respect so I may see that I and all things are One.

--Amen

THE GIFT OF SAFETY

As contrary as it may seem, our safety lies not in what we keep out, but in what we are willing to let in. All our attempts at safety have been to keep out. But what we fail to realize is that what we keep out—we also keep in, for our focus lies on what we fear.

And we have tried to keep out many things. We thought our safety lay in keeping out certain feelings or any feeling at all. We thought our safety lay in keeping out any thoughts of what frightened us. We thought our safety lay in protecting ourselves from experiences and circumstances that scared us and brought back old helpless memories, old feelings of unworthiness and pain. We thought our safety lay in keeping out people who might harm us, and soon we became afraid of almost everyone.

We thought our safety lay in the controls we could keep, but all our controls had one thing in mind—to keep out everything that would threaten any sense of security.

And the more we tried to keep our world safe, the more hostile our environment seemed to become. The more we tried to manage safety, the more we tried to keep out what seemed to consume us—the more barricades we had to erect, the more locks we had to use, the more armor we had to wear, and the more feelings we had to suppress.

The gift of Safety takes us in a direction we have not wanted to go, for we thought our safety came from running away rather than looking into our fears. The gift of Safety takes us on a journey to the very heart of our fears so we may watch them dissolve and be replaced with all things loving, with all things supportive, with all things innocent.

The gift of Safety is the gift of Light that is shone on all our feelings of pain, attack, and revenge.

Our safety lies in letting all illusion in, so we may be finally shown the truth. We have been terrified by shadows, but no shadow can withstand the Light of God's Safety.

The gift of Safety is taking the hand of God and showing Him what frightens us the most. In safety He stands beside us and says:

> *"My child, there is another way of seeing this. I will give you My Vision. My child, there is another way of overcoming this. I will give you My Strength. There is nothing My Love will not dissolve.*
>
> *Let us look at everything that has ever brought you pain or fear, and together let us watch My Love heal each feeling you carry.*
>
> *Let us watch My Love change every thought that has ever hurt you.*
>
> *Let us see each experience through the Light of My Forgiveness.*
>
> *Let us greet each circumstance through the Light of My Caring and through the Wisdom of My Guidance.*
>
> *Let us walk together and invite all of Life in so that all that is left is a blessing for each gift we will receive.*
>
> *My child, I Am your Safety and your Safety is being Home with Me.*
>
> *Let us let everything in so only what is loving and what is innocent remains.*
>
> *Let Me hold your hand so you may understand where Your Safety lies."*

THE GIFT OF SEEING THE GIFT IN EACH SITUATION

There are many situations that we have found difficult. There are many situations that we have sought to avoid and resist. There are some things that have happened that we have been unable to see any purpose for. They have confused us, annoyed us, angered us, and made us fearful. There are many situations that we have judged as boring and useless. We have judged that certain situations shouldn't have happened, should not happen, and should not continue to happen.

If a situation has not gone our way, we have been unhappy and have resisted it. If things weren't going our way, then we failed to see the purpose of them.

We may avoid, we may resist, we may try to change, and we may judge whatever happens to us, but in all of these things we are not open to seeing the gift in these situations.

The gift of seeing the gift in each situation allows us to see that whatever happens is in our best interests. This gift gets our judgment out of the way so that the best can occur and be given to us.

The true gift that is present in any situation will always be to see the love beyond what appears to be happening. The gift of seeing the gift in all situations takes us beyond appearances to the real Truth and purpose beyond what we perceive. This gift heals our judgments, our conclusions, our fears, and all that we have sought to be right about.

If we are focussed on how things should be in all situations, we will be frustrated and unhappy with what is happening. If we look for the gift in each situation, then we are open to healing, to peace, and to acceptance of the Gift that is truly there.

The gift of seeing the gift makes it even simpler, for it is a reminder that this gift is given and by ourselves we have been unable to see the gift in most situations.

If we are looking with condemnation, we will see nothing to be grateful for. If we ask to see the gift, then we may be shown gratitude to go beyond wherever we are.

When we are looking for gifts, we are looking for healing and with this willingness will all our situations of fear and despair be dissolved.

We are not being asked to learn lessons—lessons of harshness and punishment. We are not being asked to accept situations of pain and abuse. We are asking for the seeing of God's gentle love, gentle guidance, and gentle connection. We are asking to see our Higher Power walking beside us each step of the way. We are asking to see the gift of going beyond all our judgments in each situation.

The gift of seeing the gift in each situation puts us in touch with the unfoldment of what is most appropriate for us and our happiness.

Prayer:

Dear Higher Power, I fail to see the gift in this situation.

Please show me Love's presence even here. I do not wish to be in this situation.

Please show me the gift so it may be released. I'm afraid of this situation, please show me the gift of Your Vision so that the fears may be seen beyond.

Please show me that the gift in each situation is You showing me the gift in each situation.

--Amen

THE GIFT OF SEEING WHAT I HAVE TO GIVE

At times we feel quite empty. We don't have any patience to give. We don't have any wisdom. We do not wish to give our time to listen to any more problems. At times we are tired of giving and cannot come up with anything more to give.

Quite often, we judge what we have to give. We judge what value could come from us. How could anything that we have to give be worth something to someone else?

We are both afraid to give, for fear of being sucked dry, and we are afraid that what we give will never be good enough. We are afraid that the giving will never have an end, and we are conscious of the conditions of the giving. We are conscious of the resentment and the reluctance to give. And we are afraid that what we give will only expose the fraudulence of what we have to give—it will expose the worthlessness of our giving.

We don't see what we have to give. Giving impatience, anger, and resentment do not seem in short supply. But the giving of love, compassion, and understanding seem mostly beyond our power.

The gift of seeing what I have to give is first to see the Source of all giving. We feel empty when we believe we must come up with the giving. We feel drained when we believe we must manufacture what we have to give.

The gift of seeing what I have to give is the gift of seeing that God gives us everything. He is the Giver of all giving. When we allow the giving to be given to us, we will always have something to give. Our giving is limited, but the gift of giving comes from a limitless Source.

The gift of seeing what I have to give is truly seeing that we have this gift of giving within us. We need not maintain it. We need only ask for the well-spring of its presence.

The gift of seeing what I have to give is also the sharing of wherever we are without judgment. We let people see us. We let people see when we are letting go, when we are having difficulties, when we are in joy, and when we are in pain. The gift of letting people see us is part of what we have to give, for it is the gift of ourselves.

All that we have to give are gifts from the heart. They are gifts of who we are and who our Higher Power is. The gift of seeing what I have to give is the gift of seeing that our Higher Power is always with us expressing the giving. It is the gift of seeing that what we give is our own innocence, our own beauty, our own wisdom, our own expression of all that we receive.

Question: What do I have to give?

Answer: Total honesty of where you are.

Question: Do people truly wish this?

Answer: More than anything, for this honesty allows all of us to be. This honesty allows us to go beyond where we are. This honesty opens all doors. What greater gift is there to give?

We ask God: "What do I have to give?"

We are answered:

The gift of forgiveness that is given to you.

The gift of compassion with which I see you.

The gift of seeing without judgment, with which I know you.

The gift of patience with which I hear you.

The gift of caring with which I hold you.

You may give the gift of love with which I created you.

You may give the gift of inclusion with your completeness.

You have the gift of giving of yourself in all honesty.

Everything that is Mine I give to you so you may have everything to give.

And everything you give will be your gift to Me.

THE GIFT OF SERENITY

Serenity is the gift that takes us beyond all appearances. Serenity is not protection from what disturbs us—it is that quiet sense of peace amidst what seems to be very disturbing. With the gift of Serenity, we no longer have to react with our old defensive ways. Serenity is the gift with which we see another way. It is a quiet certainty that whatever may happen, a healing solution is always possible.

Serenity cannot be touched by any doubts, resentments, or anger, for it is a gift. It is the knowledge that our Higher Power is with us constantly—walking with us and teaching us the ways of love and forgiveness. Serenity would take us beyond whatever we experience. It is that holy place where we are in touch with the strength of our Higher Power. We are serene with the knowledge of God's Will for us. We are granted Serenity—it is a gift; it is a peace, which cannot be threatened by fear, illusion, or any perception that has caused us pain.

With Serenity, we may accept God's Will for us. With Serenity we may accept God's Support and Love for us. With Serenity we may accept God's care. With Serenity we may accept there is another way.

"God grant me the Serenity..."

THE GIFT OF SHARING

To share is to open to. To share is to be with. To share is to allow another to be. To share is to come from the heart.

Truly, what we share in are all the gifts of our Higher Power. We don't share love so much as we share in the presence of Love. We share in the presence of Understanding. We share in the spirit of Compassion. We share in the moment of Truth. We share in the gift of Honesty.

We don't have to come up with what we have to share—we are the sharing. To share is to let our being come forth.

To share is to come from wherever we are without having to judge it. To share is to invite another to be in God's Presence.

We share our fears, so the light may enter. We share our tears, so that our pain may dissolve. We share our expression, so that we might be heard. We share our story, so that others may find answers. We share our weakness, so we may find our strength. We share our doubts, so we may be given solutions. We share our hearts, so we may see our innocence. We share ourselves, so we may find peace.

Truly, the gift of Sharing shows us the oneness we all share in. The gift of Sharing allows us to see ourselves in each one with whom we share.

The gift of Sharing allows us to let in another so we may see our own reflection. The gift of Sharing shows us how to simply listen while another becomes in touch with their inner wisdom.

The gift of Sharing is the gift of being—we share our being. We share in the presence of being totally alive. We share in the presence of Light. We share in the presence of Wonder. We allow the gift of Sharing to show us what we need to say and to give us patience in our listening.

To share is to invite. We invite all of God's gifts into our lives, and we invite others to join in this Presence. We share who we are and we share Who our Higher Power is. We share our honesty and our truth. We share in wholeness and we share in completeness. We share in the treasures that are given to us each time we would wish to share their beauty. We share in God's Presents.

Each gift that is shared is returned one-hundred-fold.

Each loving thought that is shared heals many times over, for ultimately, only what is true can be shared.

We share the illusions we hold, because we wish the Truth.

We share our fears and tears, because we wish the comfort of others once again.

We share our doubts, because we want another way.

We share our lack of faith, because we want the faith that is honest and real.

We share our anger, because we no longer wish to keep it—we wish release.

We share our pain, because we wish healing.

And with sharing we are connected—connected to our wholeness, connected to all things, and connected with our Source.

THE GIFT OF SHARING HAPPINESS

All gifts of God are eternally present. The gifts do not disappear; they only await our invitation; they only await our willingness to ask.

The gift of Happiness does not disappear when we are fearful or sad. We do not lose happiness—only our awareness of it. It is only to be remembered that happiness is a gift. We cannot make ourselves happy. We cannot make others happy, nor can they make us happy. But we can ask for the presence of this gift, and in this asking do we share happiness with each other.

The gifts of God include everyone. There are no exceptions—we are all given an opportunity to receive these gifts. It is for this reason that we cannot help but share happiness when we are in touch with the gift of Happiness. We share an opportunity for others to ask for, and receive this gift also.

We do not experience the gift of Happiness alone. This gift opens us to all of Life. It lets us touch and be touched by the Life that is all around us.

The gift of sharing happiness is a gift of inclusion, for we are only truly happy when we are sharing the gift of Love, the gift of Joy, the gift of Happiness with others.

Even when others are not physically present, the gift of sharing happiness reconnects us with them. It brings us remembrance of Oneness and of truly seeing the gift of those who are in our lives.

The gift of sharing happiness is a realization that this gift is within us, that it won't go away, and that we need only ask to be blessed by its presence once again. It is a realization that the true nature of our being expresses the happiness at being Who we are and our happiness in discovering ourselves in each other. "There by the grace of God go I," is the dawning of this gift. We share life with all things, for ultimately, in sharing happiness we are all things—we are in touch with the gift of Oneness.

The gift of sharing happiness is the freedom we experience when we allow that inner Source, that Higher Wisdom to guide us.

Truly, to be happy is to be with God, for that is the Source of our well of being, of our well of happiness, and in God are all things shared and are all things in touch with the happiness of their being.

The gift of sharing happiness is the gift of finding ourselves, for when we share the gifts that are within us, we find these gifts reflected back in the vast expanse of our being.

With God I am all things.
With God I am all being.
Let us celebrate this.
Let us share this in this moment of joy and happiness.

The sharing is the happiness.
The happiness is the sharing.

We are in touch with the Presence in the presents. When we share in that, we all are gifted children.

Be present to enjoy the Presence.

THE GIFT OF SIMPLICITY

We, with our self-will, have complicated life to the point of desperation and chaos. All our solutions have been complex indeed with many ramifications and consequences, but we soon find that any of our solutions, however complicated and involved they may be—go nowhere.

We find, now, that we are given a very simple solution—we are given the solution of a Higher Power. We are given a solution of a simple Program. We are given the gift of Simplicity.

Simplicity is not tunnel vision, nor is it a lack of intelligence or knowing. The truly simple life has All-Knowing and understanding. It allows in everything—all ideas, awareness, and perception. The gift of Simplicity, then, is a gift that guides us to a simple solution amidst all answers and all direction. To simplify is not to exclude, it is to allow in everything so that the best answer may be given.

With our Higher Power in charge of our lives, obtaining the best answers and the most appropriate solutions becomes simple. The direction becomes clear. What is for everyone's highest good becomes evident.

The gift of Simplicity is the gift of our Higher Power, for with our Higher Power all answers are simply to let in more Peace and more Joy into our lives. The gift of simplicity is a simple solution—the solution of our Higher Power.

THE GIFT OF SOBRIETY

Many alcoholics have long suffered from the affliction of alcoholism. They have been unable to stop drinking. They have been unhappy and they have caused much unhappiness. They have had great intentions of quitting drinking, but these intentions indeed paved the way to hell. They were lost, hopeless, and dis-eased. Alcohol ran their lives and blinded them to any gifts that they either had to give or to receive.

The gift of Sobriety is indeed a precious gift, for we realize that the alcoholic cannot heal himself alone. He needs the help of others with this gift and he needs the help of a Power greater than his addiction.

The gift of Sobriety opens up a whole new life free from addiction, free from hopelessness, and free from despair. It is the gift that comes with the realization: "I cannot do this alone...God help me!"

It seems that the gift of Sobriety is not applicable for all of us. Some of us do not have a problem with drinking, some us have never been attracted to drinking. But we say: the gift of Sobriety goes beyond the freedom from drinking. The gift that is given to the alcoholic is given to us all whether we suffer from this affliction or not. The gift of Sobriety promises release from any addiction. It promises release from a life run on self-will. It promises being able to live without using—whether it be alcohol, drugs, anger, victimization, hurt, relationships...

The gift of Sobriety is for all of us. If we are addicted to a behavior, to a belief, to an outcome—this gift will set us free. If we are stuck in using the same words, patterns, thoughts, and feelings, this gift will release us.

If we have always had the gift of Sobriety in terms of alcohol, we may be grateful that we have not had the struggle of the alcoholic. We may wish to ask that others still suffering from this dis-ease receive this gift. We have this gift and in having it, we may ask that our friends, family, and strangers receive it also.

The gift of Sobriety is the gift that takes us beyond what we cannot let go of. It shows us we are not alone. It shows us we may ask for help for whatever consumes us. It shows us others who have walked the dark journey of an addiction and have come into the light. It shows us there is another way of living beyond any insanity we may experience in our lives.

With the gift of Sobriety we are no longer impaired with what we seek or use to control our lives with. The gift of Sobriety is the gift of another way—our Higher Power's Way.

The gift of Sobriety is a promise that we will not be left alone and afraid in our struggle to overcome our fears, our worst demons, our own private hells. It is a promise of a gift of help, of solutions. It is a promise that there is Someone Who walks beside us even in our darkest moments. It is a promise of reconnection with light and direction. It is a promise of being able to live free from darkness, free from addiction, and free from what we have created.

Truly, to sober up is to wake up. We wake up to the light of our Higher Power. We wake up to another way. We wake up to freedom and release.

THE GIFT OF SOLUTIONS

"Do you want to be right or do you want a solution?" It seems that what we want to be right about is the solution. We believe it is the only answer and defend it as the solution that will save us. But we finally see: Anytime that we want to be right, we do not wish a solution, for ultimately we would rather be right about our solution than the possibility of the most appropriate solution.

When we want to be right, we will not hear any answers, for we have decided what will make us happy and we have decided no other way is possible.

What we are right about is all our old perceptions, conclusions, proofs, and beliefs about the world. So determined are we to see our version of the world as true that we are not open to another way. We do not wish a solution; we only wish to be right.

We can be open to solutions, but if we become right about them, we have closed off the possibility of all solutions.

Anytime there is conflict, we will find ourselves being right, and as long as we are being right, there can be no solution. The answer is not to find ourselves in the wrong, nor is it to be subservient to our true selves. It is merely a consideration which says:

> *"I'm willing to give over to my Higher Power what I am wanting to be right about here in order that He may give me the most healing solutions."*

We finally see that when we are right, we are in charge. When we are willing to release what we are right about, the most appropriate solution can always be given.

So entrenched are we in being right about our solutions that we have sometimes not seen it is that wanting to be right which blocks all solutions.

"Do you want to be right or do you want a solution?" We are asked to consider that perhaps solutions are to be found by releasing what we defend so strenuously as being right.

THE GIFT OF SPONTANEITY

Often we have acted on impulse and later regretted it. Sometimes we have our lives planned down to the last detail with scarcely any room to breathe. It seems that the alternative has been to live somewhere between these two extremes.

We've acted without thinking. We've done or said whatever has come into out minds without thinking. We've acted suddenly and rashly. And we have gone to the other extreme. We have tried to regulate our lives so that everything was known beforehand and strictly adhered to.

The gift of Spontaneity is not a gift that acts on impulse. It is not a gift that encourages us to act rashly or without thinking. The gift of Spontaneity is truly the gift of being in touch with how we feel and where we are coming from. With the gift of Spontaneity we are in touch with what we wish to express, with what we would like to ask and to open to. Truly, spontaneity is being in touch with the moment and responding to the now. Spontaneity, then, is the expression of living in the now.

The gift of Spontaneity is not a lack of plans, nor a resistance to having plans. It is simply a willingness to give our plans over to our Higher Power, so that the spirit of life may come through in the most healing and appropriate way. It is a willingness to allow life's flow to come through these plans or any other direction that leads us to live fully each moment.

We may have plans, but with the gift of Spontaneity, we're open to letting go of these plans so that the spirit of unfoldment may lead us to be more in touch with who we are and more in touch with the Source within us.

Truly, the more in touch with ourselves we are-- the more spontaneous we become. The more aware we are of what we wish to express and ask—the more we are willing to let life unfold.

When we do not trust, when we are not in touch with our Higher Power, we are apt to try to control all aspects of our lives. We are so busy planning and protecting the future that spontaneity is not possible.

The gift of Spontaneity puts us in touch with the gift of Trust and Faith in our Higher Power. We are in touch with the guidance that flows each time we let God give us direction. We are open to Life's unfoldment—we are open to the gift of Spontaneity.

Quite often, our spontaneity or expression of life is squelched when we become self-conscious. When we are in the ego, when we have E dged G od O ut, our spontaneity is severely limited. But, the gift of Spontaneity is truly Self-Consciousness.

We live in the spirit of our Higher Power. We live in the spirit of the moment. With the gift of Spontaneity, we are in touch with all life around us—we are in touch with what is appropriate each moment.

We express the Now.

THE GIFT OF STARTING WHERE I AM WITHOUT JUDGMENT

Very rarely do we like where we are. We have many judgments on where we are coming from and how we are being. We have resistance to feeling what we are feeling. We have doubt about those things we are doing. We have frustration at times with our progress. We see—"This is where I am, but THAT is where I should be. I shouldn't be where I am here!"

In recovery, it is important for us to receive the gift of starting where we are without judgment. For only by starting where we are without judgment can we recover from the constant judgment, disapproval, and anger we have directed at ourselves. It becomes impossible to BE without this gift. It becomes impossible to feel and express without this gift. If we resist and judge where we are, then we cannot begin in peace and acceptance to let in another way.

What if we did not have to judge where we were, how we felt, what we thought, what we did? What a gift! For when we do not judge, we may let go and begin again. When we do not judge, there is forgiveness and we may go beyond wherever we are to be in touch with all the gifts we have to give.

Yes, we come from many strange places, and in our recovery feel many strange things. We may come from judgment and hatred. We may start with the same old patterns and desperations. We may feel, "Oh no, not again!—I thought I dealt with this already." We may be in difficult financial circumstances. We may use familiar old controls and manipulations, but the beauty of the gift of starting where we are without judgment is that we no longer have to judge. We are ready for a new beginning. We are ready for another way. With this gift we go beyond judgment. With this gift we can start from wherever we are without the burden of judgment and condemnation. With this gift we begin from wherever we are with acceptance and with the knowledge that there is a better way.

If we did not have to judge, what could we not begin?

If we did not have to condemn where we were starting from, then our journey of recovery could begin immediately. This gift is the first step on our journey Home—the journey that would bring us in touch with ourselves.

Not judging ourselves does not mean we ignore or deny what we have been doing. We admit exactly what we have been using, exactly how we have been controlling. The difference is, we no longer have to stay stuck in judgment—we can live our lives in a better, kinder and more loving way.

THE GIFT OF STRENGTH

We thought that our strength lay in the quality and the quantity of the defenses we used. We thought that our strength lay in the denial and suppression of our feelings. We thought that our strength lay in not showing our hurt and our confusion. We thought that strength lay in holding on until we could hold on no longer. We thought that strength lay in doing it ourselves, in going it alone, in being independent. We thought our strength lay in pushing and effort. We thought that our strength lay in fighting, struggle, and conflict.

We thought our strength lay in our own devices and ways of making others be there for us. We thought our strength lay in a total lack of emotion, in a world totally devoid of support and caring. We thought our strength lay in keeping up our guard and suspicion. We thought our strength lay in learning all the right moves, all the right jargon, and all the right people. We thought our strength lay in being able to anticipate and control whatever happened. We thought our strength lay in our self-will, in our good intention, in our ability to hold fast to our beliefs, to all we were right about.

However, in this list of what we consider strength, we will notice that in this context, strength means control. We have thought strength came from what we were able to control. But we are seeing the great cost that occurs whenever we try to control anything. There is nothing that will drain strength faster than control. We finally see that perhaps strength is not holding on to—it is letting go of.

The gift of Strength, as with all other gifts, is the gift of our Higher Power's Strength. We have not seen the strength of love, for "our" strength would keep love out. Our strength is dependent on what we keep out, not what we let in. With our strength, we cannot let in the gifts of God, for our strength sees receiving any gifts as weakness.

We ask for the gift of God's Strength to let go of all our barriers, all our walls, all our blocks to receiving true strength—the gift of Strength.

True strength lets in love, lets in caring, lets in support. The gift of Strength does not despise feelings, but allows us to express them, gives us strength to show them.

The gift of Strength sees itself not in defense, but in letting in the gift of Strength. When we defend, we can neither give nor receive gifts—we can only keep in or keep out.

The gift of Strength shows us the strength in gentleness—gentleness for where we are, gentleness for what we feel, gentleness for what we fear, and the strength to go beyond all these illusions.

The gift of Strength shows that our strength is not in holding on to our controls, but in letting go of them.

The gift of Strength is the gift with which we may let go to our Higher Power. With this gift we have the strength to feel, to open, to share, to live, to comfort, to let in, and most of all, the strength to be.

Prayer:

My strength has really been weakness. It has come from fear and desperation.

Your Strength comes from love and acceptance.

Your Strength comes from letting in everything so that Your Awareness may dissolve all that has caused me pain.

Your Strength is in nurturing. My "strength" has been in loneliness and separation.

Your Strength would include all gifts. My strength would deny and block them.

Please let Your Strength flow through me so I may have the strength of honesty, opening, and acceptance.

--Amen

THE GIFT OF SUPPORT

We have tried to support ourselves and we were never quite sure we could do so for any length of time. We have tried to find others to support us and have been angry and disappointed when they were unable to care for us as we thought we should be supported. We expected support and saw the futility of receiving it from certain people. We demanded support and were refused. We tried to make people support us and were constantly disillusioned. We even rejected support when it did not come in a form we had anticipated. We rejected support fearing the strings attached to it. We rejected support because it had come too late. We rejected support because we wanted to prove we could do it ourselves without the assistance of anyone.

We demanded support and, often in the same breath, we rejected it. Support has been a very touchy area, for we have wanted others to look after us, but we did not want to admit this and above all we wanted to supervise how, when, and how much support should be given and in what form it should come.

But most of all, we feared having to be the support, because we did not know how. We tried to avoid supporting or we smothered others with our "support" hoping they would not find out about our inadequacies.

We have wished guarantees for support that were always unfulfilled. We could not trust support, for always were we disappointed—others were not always there to support us.

The gift of Support finally releases us from one very destructive concept. Very simply—we cannot make anyone support us. We cannot make them be there for us or support us in any way. Now this may seem like the bad news, but it is really our release. No, we cannot really make anyone support us, but support can still come through these people when we finally give up how it should come.

The gift of Support is a gift that gives us support beyond our management. We are in a sea of support—it is all around us. But we are drowning in despair because we are still holding on to the iron weight that we think would save us. We are still hanging on to how support should come—we forget to see, we forget to let in the support that is there in a million different ways.

The gift of Support widens our vision so we may see and receive the support that is everywhere. No, we cannot make the universe support us, but the gift of Support will be the gift of letting in the flow of support that is continual.

The only true support comes from our Higher Power. We cannot make anyone give us this support, nor can we by ourselves be a support. But our Higher Power is the Support working through others and working through ourselves.

Our Higher Power is the gift of Support that we will have to give. Truly, the gift of Support is received when we allow our Higher Power to be the support in our lives—not ourselves and our controls, not our expertise, not our wealth or poverty, not our manipulations of illness, not our making others be there for us, not our demanding, but our willingness to let our Higher Power be the gift of Support.

Our Higher Power's gift of Support frees us from our desperations and from our frustrations. We can finally admit that in our relationships we do not know how to support but we are willing to let the gift of Support enter through us, through others, or through any other appropriate vehicle that our Higher Power would use. We no longer have to manufacture support or demand how it will be given.

The gift of Support is the knowledge of our Higher Power's care for us in all that we do. We no longer have to get support—we ask for the gift of Support so this may be expressed in all areas of our lives.

Prayer:

Higher Power, let me be an expression of Your Support.

Let me see Your Support coming through others.

Let me see Your Support in all circumstances.

Help me to receive Your Support beyond all that I value, beyond the form I would have Support take.

Would You be the Support I have to give.

Would You help me receive Your Support by helping me admit I do not know what is best for my support.

Would You be the Support with which I receive Your Support.

--Amen

When we realize each attribute of God is a gift, it becomes much easier to accept whatever the gift may happen to be. So often, we believe that we are responsible for manufacturing Love, Trust, Faith, Truth, Support. But when we see that each gift is present already; is simply waiting to be given, we will be able to accept without first having to "make it".

To the degree that we think we are responsible for getting or making support in our lives, will be the degree we will be reluctant to accept Support in all areas. By ourselves we are unable, ultimately, to support anyone or anything. We forget that it is a gift, not something that we have to come up with.

If we were to ask ourselves would we truly wish to support another unconditionally, we would be overwhelmed with fear, for how would this be possible? How could we do this? But with the gift of Support, comes the unconditional giving of this gift. We no longer have the condition that we must produce support; we only have the willingness to accept this gift from our Higher Power.

This gift may come through us, this gift may come from around us. But, the true Source of this gift is our Higher Power. And as our Higher Power is all around us, so is the gift of Support that He would give to us.

This gift is not conditional. It has no strings attached. Our Higher Power does not require us to earn this gift, nor deserve it. He does not require us to know how to give it. It is the gift He is willing to give when we ask for His Support in any situation.

We have been reluctant to give our support because we thought we had to somehow come up with enough of it. With the gift of Support, we may be willing to ask for, and express this gift in all areas.

The gift of Support is truly support for Who we are. It is support for our being. It is support to live and let live. It is support to nourish and be nourished. It is the support of encouragement. It is the support of solutions. But most of all, it is the awareness that our Higher Power has never left us, nor will He desert us now. It is the support of knowing God is present. It is the support of being able to let in the gifts for our support. It is the support that gives us courage. It is the support that surrounds us with our Higher Power's Love. Truly, support is the foundation of our Higher Power under us, around us, and within us.

We are supported by Life—it is a gift.

We are supported in all abundance—it is a gift.

We are supported by unlimited receiving—this is a gift.

We are supported in all that we have to give—it is a gift.

"Please give me the gift of Support to unconditionally give Your Support. Please give me the gift of Support to unconditionally receive Your Support."

We have tried to prove:

"I can do it myself—I'll show you.
I can do it myself—don't help me.
I can do it myself—let me show you how you can do it too.
I can do it myself—I don't need anything from you.
I can do it myself—no thank you.
I can do it myself...so where are You?"

Instead we may see:

"I can do it myself—but with You the best can be done.
I can do it myself—but I don't have to do it alone anymore.
I can do it myself—but I like the support that comes when I am open to receive.
I can do it myself—but I like it when I am in Your Care.
I can do it myself—but I like the connectedness that happens when we are together.
I can do it myself—but by myself I cannot receive Your gifts. Would You please include me in Your gifts, so I may see the gift of myself in You."

The ability to be able to receive is support.

How easy are you to give to? If you are difficult to give to, then you will also have difficulty with support.

The freedom to receive is support.

The choice to receive is support.

As long as we, through fear, try to control what we receive, to that extent we cannot receive in freedom, we cannot receive with choice, we cannot receive with support—we cannot receive. The gift of allowing God into our lives is Support.

THE GIFT OF SUPPORTIVE FRIENDS

These are the friends who have seen past our futile attempts to hide our defects and our weaknesses. They have seen our petty ways and they have seen our lack of forgiveness. They have seen our insecurities and they know most of our dark secrets that we have tried to keep hidden and forgotten. Yet, having seen all these things, they see only our true essence beyond all our controls and are still our friends.

These are the friends we have sometimes gotten angry at and we have told them to go away and never darken our doorstep again. These are the friends who will let us away with nothing and in the depth of their love, these are the friends who will say "no" to what we try to control and manipulate.

These are the friends who will risk telling us of their own fears and insecurities because they wish no block to come between the realness and Honesty in the relationship. These are the friends who have seen us at the height of our controls and with all our masks in place. But these are the friends who see past all our commotions to who we truly are. It is our realness they want and it is their openness they wish to give.

Supportive friends are the friends with whom we can be and with whom we can hide, knowing that they can see our being anyway. These friends are really us in all our reflections, desires, and willingness. It is us we see and it is us they reflect. These are the friends we can see our true being in and with these friends we walk the journey Home.

The gift of having and being a supportive friend comes from God. For it is God's Love and God's Caring that we invite into any relationship and with these gifts is the relationship a holy one.

THE GIFT OF TAKING MYSELF LIGHTLY

We take everything so seriously. We take our appearance seriously and try to improve it. We take our conversations seriously and try to upgrade them. We take our work seriously and keep our nose to the grindstone. We take our friendships seriously and keep track of what we owe and what is owed to us. We take our relationships seriously and work on them, trying to keep them together. We take the world seriously and predict gloom and catastrophe. We take our health seriously and either work hard to maintain it, or give up in despair because our addictions seem just too much for us. We take our faith seriously and seek to defend it. We take our parenting seriously and become firm and unyielding in what we think is right. We take our spiritual programs seriously and give ourselves a bad time when we do not follow the principles in a serious manner. We take life seriously and monitor our progress. But at the root of all this seriousness is us—taking ourselves seriously.

The gift of taking ourselves lightly is a very healing gift, for it allows us to let go. It allows us to let go of how the world should be and how we should be. We are able to take ourselves lightly because our Higher Power is given all our responsibilities, all our burdens, all our heaviness, all our seriousness to allow us to live in His Light.

With the gift of taking ourselves lightly, we let go of how things should be and are open to the lightness of our Higher Power's way.

The gift of taking ourselves lightly is the gift of being able to laugh at our mistakes, knowing they will be gently corrected. We are even able to laugh at our seriousness.

The gift of taking ourselves lightly is the gift of being able to observe the situations we are in without having to get caught up in them, without having to take them so seriously. We are given a moment when light can enter. We are given a moment when we no longer have to react in the old, rigid ways. We are given a moment when we can see a choice, when we can see another way.

The gift of taking ourselves lightly is the gift that acknowledges that what we have made is not real, nor is it permanent—our Higher Power may always heal whatever we have done so seriously and bring His light and laughter to shine upon it.

The gift of taking ourselves lightly is the gift that releases the stranglehold on doing things our way. If we are taking ourselves lightly, we are open to the most appropriate solutions; we are open to how things may be resolved with ease.

The gift of taking ourselves lightly is the gift of seeing ourselves with compassion, with laughter, with gentleness, and with healing, through our Higher Power's eyes.

Prayer:

Would You please be the light with which I may be taken lightly.

Would You help me look upon myself and my efforts with Your Wisdom.

Would You help me see others and their "seriousness" with compassion.

Would You help me "lighten-up".

--Amen

"Angels fly because they take themselves lightly."

Anytime you put yourself on a judgment scale—even one to ten—you still come out heavy.

THE GIFT OF TEARS

We have cried many tears and we have stuffed many tears, because it was not safe to cry. We have hidden our tears, used our tears, and been unable to experience tears. All of these tears have been tears of loneliness and desperation.

The gift of tears is the gift of release and connection. These tears connect us with the fountain of youth. These tears are tears of relief and joy that we are no longer alone. These tears are the tears that let our inner child find expression once more. These are tears of renewal—we renew our youth; we renew our connection with each other; we renew our connection with Life.

These are tears, not of bitterness, but of sharing. These are tears, not of weakness, but of strength. These are tears where laughter is not far behind.

The gift of tears is the gift of being able to feel again, and the gift of finding all love and oneness again. These are the tears that will dissolve all our masks of pretense and fear. These are the tears that come from a well-spring of innocence. These are the tears of a Holy remembrance. These are the tears of a faith that was never lost and of a life that has never died. These are the tears that bring us home to our Higher Power's comfort once more.

THE GIFT OF TRUE CHRISTMAS

We have sought long and hard to give the most appropriate gift. We have wanted to make others happy and we have wanted to show our love through the gifts we gave. We wanted to prove our caring through giving gifts and we became desperate when all the gifts we chose never seemed to quite express our true desire.

Sometimes we became discouraged with the commotion of Christmas gift giving and we resented and resisted the emptiness these gifts and commotions seemed to symbolize. We did not know what to give. We did not know what was appropriate. We did not know how to make others happy. It all seemed so meaningless.

At Christmas we found it difficult to receive. Had we given the right gift at the right price in order to receive what was given to us? Had we given a gift that was worth far more than what we received? And by receiving it, were we being taken advantage of? What if we received nothing and thus were aware that we were not cared for? What if we did not have enough to give and could not afford the giving? What if what we were given only showed how disconnected we truly were from those around us?

There seemed to be much confusion around Christmas giving and receiving. How do we become suddenly close with those we never understood and who never seemed to understand us? How do we suddenly feel joy and connectedness where there has been distance and resentment? How do we give when we ourselves feel uncertain and fearful? How do we receive when there is guilt that we have not done our best?

We looked at Christmastime with hope and dread—hope that our emptiness would be filled and dread that we may be left empty once again. Hope that we may find connectedness, and dread that our loneliness would only be intensified.

The gift of true Christmas is not a gift we provide, although it may be expressed through us and around us. It is a gift that does the giving, does the receiving, does the connecting, and brings about the opening to all these things. Yes, we reach the point where we have nothing to give. We reach the point where we are unable to receive. But with this acknowledgment, comes the gift of giving and receiving—the gift of true Christmas.

The gift of true Christmas is the gift of the Christ within, where all giving and receiving begins. It is the gift of connection with God, Who brings about all other connections. It is a gift we cannot find by ourselves, but it is given to us. It is a gift we might not know how to receive, but it will be received for us.

The gifts of true Christmas come in unlimited ways—they come with our hearts and our joy of being together. They come with our love to open in understanding with those around us. They come with acceptance and gratitude of each other. They come with humility that the true gift of Christmas is far beyond what we have so desperately tried to provide and just as desperately tried to get. It is the spirit of Christmas, the spirit of Peace and Oneness that is expressed through whatever we are open to give and receive. It is the spirit of opening to a far greater vision and possibility of connection than we could ever dream possible. It is the spirit of blessings—we are blessed with God's spirit, we are blessed with this moment to share.

It is a day of recognition that God's gift of the Christ within us is here eternally and is constantly given to us. It is a day of gratitude and remembrance that God's gifts are ours and we need only ask to be aware of them. It is a day of celebration, for it is our own birth—the birth of another way, the birth of acceptance of our worth, the birth of our connection with our Source. It is a day of renewal, a day of opportunities for healing with those closest to us. It is a day of inclusion, the including of all living things into the circle of our Higher Power's love.

The gift of true Christmas is your gift—let it be given to you today.

God's gifts will never disappoint us.

THE GIFT OF TRUST

We have thought we had to trust many things, but we did not trust any of them. We have felt that we had to trust people, circumstances, and yet we found this fearful, for trust only seemed to open us to more hurt and pain. Most often, what we trusted in left us disappointed and disillusioned. We have tried to manufacture trust and have felt more distrustful than ever. Each thing or person we have trusted has seemed to let us down in one way or another. There is a scared child within us very fearfully saying: "I'm afraid to trust!"

We are offered the gift of God's Trust. This is a gift we'll be unable to make or manufacture ourselves. God's gift of Trust does not require that we trust anyone or anything. This is very important, for we have thought that to be on the spiritual path, we had to come up with trust for each person and circumstance. We are told—"You are not required to trust anyone or anything. You are only required to trust that whatever you give to your Higher Power will always result in what is most healing, and for ultimate happiness and freedom."

The gift of Trust allows us to see that our Higher Power's Will for us is Peace and Joy. The gift of Trust is a gift that tells us whatever person or circumstance we give to our Higher Power, whatever relationship we ask Him to heal—the most appropriate action and direction will occur. In other words: the gift of Trust finally allows us to see that what we trust in, is our Higher Power working through each person and each circumstance for our healing. We trust that what is turned over to our Higher Power is resolved. We trust that what we turn over to our Higher Power will find the most appropriate solution. We trust that whatever relationship we turn over to our Higher Power will find an answer of healing and of forgiveness.

The gift of Trust, then, is really the gift of Certainty with our Higher Power. It is this gift of Certainty with which Trust is given. We are not required to trust each other. We trust that when we turn the relationship over to the Higher Power, the best will always occur.

We do not trust in this world, for it is insane. But we do trust in our Higher Power working through this world. We do not trust in our own strength, but we do trust in the Strength of our Higher Power working through us.

Whatever we give over, we trust will be healed. We trust that giving our will over to the care of our Higher Power will always bring a life with Ease, a life of purpose, and a life of connection. We trust that when we ask, the gifts will always be for our release from whatever has caused us pain and fear.

In this are all things held in Trust—God's Trust.

THE GIFT OF TRUTH

The truth we have sought has needed much defense. Sometimes we have had a glimpse of the Truth and proceeded to erect mighty barriers to contain it. We have protected our "truth" at a very high cost, for to protect anything, much defense and separation is needed. We have sought to hold on to our truth and to convince others of its reality. But our truth seemed very evasive. We would believe one thing to be true, only to find that perhaps the opposite was true as well. We thought truth to be very confusing. What we believed we thought was true, and what others believed had to be false. And if we happened to see some truth in what they believed—it frightened us and only made us defend our truth more strenuously.

So disillusioned were we, at times, with truth that it seemed safer to believe that nothing was true. And so, we looked for truth, found a glimpse of truth, defended it, and lost sight of it. Our truth was a limited search indeed.

The Gift of Truth from our Higher Power is a gift which encompasses everything. We can only have the Truth when we allow everything to be placed in our Higher Power's care. The Truth includes everything, for only in this can we be shown the real Truth of God's gifts. Only what is loving is true. Only what is innocent is true. The Truth would reveal the essence of our true being in God.

The Gift of Truth would show us our true connection with each other—the connection of innocence, the connection of peace and the connection of love.

God's Gift of Truth is unchanging—it has no opposite, yet it allows everything to be brought to it, so we may see past all illusions, all pain, and all separation. It is the Truth of Oneness. It is the Truth of connection. It is the Truth of loving expression. It is the Truth of Being. It is the Truth of All-Knowing.

God's Gift of Truth does not limit, nor does it separate—it is what brings us together in harmony and in acceptance. It is a Gift that needs no defence, for what is true cannot be defended. Truth does not gain its strength by exclusion. It gains its strength by its all-encompassing nature to shine away what is not loving, what is not forgiving, and what is not real. The Gift of Truth is what heals our relationships, for the Truth is: There is nothing our Higher Power cannot heal and bring together with this Gift.

THE GIFT OF UNFOLDMENT

Sometimes, we believe we must push to have things accomplished. And, of course, in order to push, we must have something to push against—opposition. And so, we push against time, people, space, deadlines, arguments, unavailability, lack, misunderstanding, and so on.

Sometimes, we take the opposite side of the coin and we wait until everything is the way we think it should be—procrastination. In order to procrastinate, we again set up opposition. We are opposed to the conditions being anything but "just right". We are opposed to beginning without certain occurrences, certain people, and the right amount of ideas, materials and overall pictures.

Whether we decide to push or to procrastinate in order to see something accomplished, we are still in a state of resistance. We are still in a state of opposition.

There is still a strong belief that, at times, we must control by either pushing or by putting off what needs to be done. Either way, there is much tension, resentment, and frustration. We seem to meet opposition at each turn.

The gift of Unfoldment opposes nothing. The gift of Unfoldment is truly allowing the natural flow to take place. The gift of Unfoldment does not have to push. Unfoldment occurs when we ask for God's Will to be done. Unfoldment keeps nothing on hold. It simply flows from one appropriate step to the next. Truly, the gift of Unfoldment is not in time at all. The gift of Unfoldment is being in the moment, which extends to include all occurrences, all solutions, and all direction.

The gift of Unfoldment is truly God's design. Those whom we need to see, we are brought in connection with. Those words that we need to hear, are brought into our awareness in the most appropriate ways. Those events that need to occur for us to be in the most healing and connected place for us, are brought into our lives.

There is a saying that there are no accidents—everything is connected. This connectedness with the support of all things is the gift of Unfoldment. Truly, when we allow this gift to be given, things occur naturally and unfold in the most healing way possible. We are literally guided by the Flow. We are led by our Higher and innermost Power.

With the gift of Unfoldment, there is no opposition. This does not mean we sit and wait, hoping that things may happen. This is still procrastination. This is still trying to control the Flow. It simply means that with the acceptance of this gift, we enter the natural flow and guidance of our Higher Power Who leads us. We find ourselves connected to those that help us on our way. We find ourselves gently guided to be where we need to be. We find ourselves giving and receiving the assistance that brings us closer to our inner power and strength.

When we truly accept the gift of Unfoldment, much is accomplished, for unfoldment is being in the heart of all connection.

Prayer:

Please give me the gift of Unfoldment so I may allow things to be and to heal in Your time.

Please give me the gift of Unfoldment so I may be connected with Your loving support which is everywhere.

Please give me the gift of Unfoldment so I may allow the beginning of whatever needs to be accomplished.

Please give me the gift of Unfoldment so I may allow all to occur with ease and gratitude.

Please give me the Wisdom to see Your Will unfolding in each situation.

Please give me the gift of Unfoldment so I may be enfolded in Your loving care and direction.

--Amen

Unfoldment is the flow of God's Will—the unfoldment of each moment into the next, with that moment connecting everything.

In letting God's Will be in each situation, we will see the gift of Unfoldment. We will see all things unfolding to bring people and situations together in healing, in harmony, and in miracles.

The gift of Tao is the gift of Unfoldment.

The gift of Love is the gift of Unfoldment.

"Thy Will be done" is the gift of Unfoldment.

"Let it be" may be rephrased to say: "Let it unfold."

THE GIFT OF USEFULNESS

We have all been taught the necessity of being useful. We have been taught that it was important to be of some use in life. But, however much we tried to be useful, the less we felt useful. Whether we tried to accomplish things or not, we often felt our efforts were useless or would be of no use.

In telling our stories of trying to control, in sharing our experiences with others, we often see just how useless our attempts to control our lives have been. We see how ineffectual our efforts at producing useful lives have been. But with the gift of usefulness that our Higher Power gives us, we find that our sharing is of much use to others in their own opening and healing. We have incredible gifts of use, but we do not make them—they are gifts. When we have tried to be of use—we used. And what we used, we abused. But we found that when we gave our lives to a Power greater than ourselves, our lives and our experience were of use once again.

There is great value that comes in sharing a life that was once run on self-will and then was turned over to our Higher Power. We are of use—not through our attempts and controls, but because we ask for God to use us in the most loving and healing way possible. We ask to be of use and in this are we given the gift of our Higher Power's Use.

The gift of Usefulness shows us the true value of everything we have ever done—when turned over to our Higher Power. There is nothing that cannot be of use for healing, if we but give it to our Higher Power for His use.

We find that with the gift of Usefulness, we have much to offer, much to give, and much to share.

What we judge is of no use to us, but what we give to our Higher Power can be used for our healing. We do not have to judge how we have lived our lives, but our lives can be given to our Higher Power so our sharing of them can be of use. The gift of Usefulness takes all we have abused and lets that very thing be used for healing and lets that very thing be the gift that is useful.

We are only of use when we are with our Higher Power—for this is the gift of Usefulness.

THE GIFT OF VISION

Our vision has been quite limited and filled with judgment. We have viewed ourselves and each other with distrust and suspicion. We have seen the world with eyes of fear and apprehension. We have seen a world of pain and disillusionment. We have seen people that did not care and that weren't there for us. We have seen situations that have had no answers and conflicts that have had no resolution. Our vision saw guilt and blame. We have seen with eyes of condemnation and judgment. We have seen ourselves as undeserving and we have seen others with eyes of jealousy and disappointment. We have seen through eyes that were blinded with pain and with fear.

We have seen the same patterns over and over again. We have looked on a world of insanity and what we have seen seems impossible to ever be healed.

We have seen disease, and we have seen with feelings of helplessness, that we could do nothing. We have seen manipulations and we have seen others as different from ourselves. We have seen attack and we were threatened by those around us. We have seen with eyes of despair that there was no way out, no release from the prison we had made.

The gift of Vision is a very precious gift indeed, for it would take us beyond all that we perceive and show us there is another way. The light of Vision would shine away all shadows that have kept us fearful. We are no longer seeing with our insane vision, for we are given the gift of our Higher Power's Vision. By ourselves, we are blind and cannot see. The brightness of our Higher Power's Vision is a gift that will allow us to truly see beyond all pain, all suffering, all grievances, and all hatred.

It is not our vision that we begin to see with—the gift of Vision would release all that has ever hurt us.

> *"God, You be my Vision today.*
> *You be the eyes with which I see today.*
> *You show me the world I will look upon today."*

The gift of Vision will show us what has always been there beyond the insanities of this world. God's Vision will show us our own innocence and the innocence of those in our lives. The gift of Vision will allow us to see the support and guidance that is all around us. The gift of Vision will show us truth, will show us the love held for us eternally.

We are given a Vision of Peace. We are given a Vision of healing. We will see with eyes of acceptance and understanding. We will see our own Worth and the truth of our own being. We will see in light, for there will be no darkness with this Vision. We will see another way—with the gift of Vision we will always see another way. We will see with the light of love. We will see all answers with the gift of our Higher Power's Vision.

THE GIFT OF VITALITY

When we speak of the gift of vitality, the first thought is that there will be strength to carry on with everyday living; there will be energy to rise above our constant burdens that we carry.

But in truth, the gift of Vitality is that joy of connection, of Life's energy running through us when we realize we have no burdens.

The gift of Vitality does not help us face life—it allows us to let the vitalness of Life come through; it allows Life to support us. In other words, when we give our burdens to our Higher Power, we are revitalized or reconnected with the strength that is His.

The gift of Vitality does not help us carry on with daily living. It is the gift that comes when our Higher Power becomes our daily living.

Our Higher Power is the "Vital" part of our lives. From this center comes vitality. Vitality is really the heart of living and the heart of living is being in touch with our Higher Power running our lives.

It is vital to put God first. Vitality is truly the gift of allowing God in. We are not given the gift of Vitality to cope with life; we are given vitality to experience life, free from pain, free from burdens and free from fear. We are not given this gift so we may have more energy to be in charge—we are recharged with that strength that comes when we give all problems to our Higher Power for His solution.

The gift of Vitality is the gift of new life each moment. It is a gift of being in touch with NOW. It is the gift of connection with all living things. We receive vitality from all around us. We live vitality and we express with vitality.

We are in touch with vitality when our whole heart is involved—when we are living, breathing, loving with all our heart. Vitality is whole-hearted living—living with all our being.

The gift of vitality is the gift of an ability to express life, to express our being. The gift of Vitality is whole-hearted in its expression, for our Higher Power is the gift of a whole heart.

It is not—"Give us some vitality so we may get on with things," it is rather—"Please take all my things that I have been wearying myself with so I may have Your Vitality." This indeed is the heart of the matter—the vital part.

THE GIFT OF WELL-BEING

We have had many judgments on our being. We have not thought well of ourselves. We have not looked at those areas where honesty was required in order to feel well with ourselves. We have not forgiven ourselves and others to feel well with the world. Our well-being has suffered from our being not being well.

The gift of well-being puts us in touch with our being and with the innocence of our being. It is a gift of acceptance. It allows us to accept where we are without judgment. It allows us to forgive and let go. It allows us peace with ourselves, and it allows us peace with others in our lives.

The gift of well-being is the gift of all being well. When we are given honesty, when we are given forgiveness and acceptance, we finally see—all is well.

There is a wellspring within us. This wellspring is our being in its true, loving and innocent nature. It is a wellspring of being. It is a gift and it is within.

The gift of well-being lets in all other gifts, for this is part of being well. When we are well, we let in love; we let in support; we let in choices that are healthy for us.

The gift of well-being is a gift that receives. And from this completeness, it is a gift that has wellness to give. With this gift we are healed, for we are in touch with our being, being well. We are in touch with our innocence and we are in touch with whatever admittance is necessary to keep us well.

Honesty is essential for our well-being—this too is a gift. Forgiveness is essential for our well-being—for it is only with forgiveness that we will see our well-being of innocence.

Being in complete freedom with others, allows more and more well-being. We are free to be and we are willing to give others the same freedom. We see more and more well-beings.

We are well in God, for God is our wellspring from which all healing flows. When we are at peace, when we are open to receiving that gift of peace—all is well. Our being is well, when all is well with our being. We allow ourselves to begin. We allow ourselves to make mistakes and to have them gently corrected. We allow ourselves love and kindness. We allow ourselves support and acceptance. We allow ourselves well-being. We allow ourselves to be.

THE GIFT OF WHOLENESS

Sometimes, it feels as if we are many different personalities. We feel alienated from ourselves and are continually surprised by the actions and reactions we have. We feel separate and cut off from knowing and trusting ourselves. In many cases, we are not connected or even on speaking terms with all of our innermost being.

There are parts of ourselves we like very much, and there are parts of ourselves that we hope will never see the light of day. There are parts of ourselves we are embarrassed by and wish to hide. There are parts of ourselves that we have numbed and forgotten. There are parts of ourselves that are still fearful and lost. There are parts of ourselves that seem to sabotage our efforts—these parts we don't understand at all. There are parts of ourselves that are clumsy and awkward. There are parts of ourselves that are very sociable and likeable. But then, there are parts of ourselves that do unkind and even destructive things—these parts do not seem socially acceptable in their behavior.

So many parts, so much separation, so much uncertainty. Which part is going to take over next? Which part will surface in our relationship today? It reaches the point where we do not trust ourselves. It reaches the point where we find ourselves our own worst enemy.

Then, there are parts of ourselves that are quite obviously separate by reason of a dis-ease condition that is most evident. There are parts of ourselves that have broken limbs. There are parts of ourselves that have sores or tumors. There are parts of ourselves that get colds and the flu. There are parts of ourselves that get weak and tired. There are parts of ourselves that are numb and ineffective. There are parts of ourselves embroiled in various emotional disturbances. There are parts of ourselves that don't see well, hear well, or feel well. Again, so many parts—so much separation.

The gift of Wholeness is really the remembering of all the parts that have been cast off and separated from us. With this gift we reconnect with all these "parts" we have been playing, so we may reclaim all that we are—the wholeness, the completeness we are.

When we were children, our behaviors, our appearance, was often judged in some way. The child that we were, the child that we still are, accepted those judgments and banished that part of itself that was not acceptable in another's eyes. We literally cut ourselves off. We cut ourselves off from our wholeness and became many "different" parts.

We are still cut off from the acceptance of many parts of ourselves. Each thing we have judged or accepted judgment about ourselves becomes something set "apart" from the awareness of our completeness. And what is cut off, cannot be healed.

Many of the diseases that we experience occur when we cut off, through judgment and condemnation, from our wholeness. In our state of disease, we often see the solution as cutting out certain parts of our body. We cut out tumors, we have bypass surgery. We apply the same solution to the part of ourselves that feels anger, sadness, hopelessness. We attempt to cut ourselves with all our many feelings—off.

The gift of Wholeness invites each part that we have condemned back into our awareness, back into acceptance, back into completeness, back into healing. The child that was judged for being angry, the part that was judged for being closed and unsociable, is invited back into our lives with full acceptance and full understanding. We begin to see that we are not bad, that our behaviors are not based on evil. They simply come from all parts of ourselves wanting to be loved, accepted, and whole.

When it is not okay for a child to express whatever it needs to express, then the child cannot release that thought, feeling, or behavior. What we judge, we become separate from—a-part from. But also, what we judge, we keep.

The gift of Wholeness allows to release all feelings of anger, frustration, fear, sadness, and even joy, so that we may become more in touch with our completeness. We may reclaim more and more of ourselves, and we will be able to do this in the spirit of forgiveness and acceptance.

With the gift of Wholeness, we discover more of ourselves and the discovery is accompanied by care and acceptance. With acceptance, anything can be released, anything can be reconnected, anything can be healed.

The gift of Wholeness is the gift of seeing that there are no parts. There is just that which has been judged and condemned. With this gift we allow all of ourselves to be. And with this allowance, comes healing.

The gift of Wholeness comes with the gift of Inclusion, for all of our being is included in being loved, heard, understood and cared for.

The gift of Wholeness does not cut away a part that has been diseased or disconnected from its source. It does not cast it off in fear and disapproval. This part, too, is invited to be heard, to give its message to help us get in "touch" with our asking. We consider including all parts to be "part" of the healing.

The usual reaction when we have a disease condition is to put a cast on it (cast-away), cut it out, cut it off, suppress it, get rid of it. We are not saying not to do these things, but we do ask you to consider what each part is expressing, asking. We do ask you to consider what each part is asking you to be in touch with—to be touched by. We do ask you to consider the gift of Wholeness.

The gift of Wholeness listens to the expression of all of us, because when we are cut off or separated from all of us, there will be an attempt to re-establish communication. The gift of Wholeness invites this.

With this gift, we begin to listen to all parts of ourselves. What is the angry child really saying? What is that closed, numb part of ourselves trying to communicate? What is the sabotage all about? What is the broken leg or tumor expressing? What about that part that thought there could never be a solution or way out of all its pain and even abuse?

The gift of Wholeness brings all parts of ourselves together in completeness and understanding. We bring ourselves fully together to find a solution—the solution of wholeness.

The gift of Wholeness is the gift of healing. And when we see our wholeness, we will see the wholeness that connects us with all things, with all solutions, with our Source.

We will enter relationships in the spirit of wholeness rather than lack. With this gift we are whole within ourselves, we are whole with each other, and we are whole within our Higher Power. We are wholly present.

The gift of Wholeness is truly being in touch with our Holiness. We are a Whole and Holy child of God.

THE GIFT OF WILLINGNESS

Such a simple gift, yet nothing can match its power. The gift of willingness is the gateway to all healing. It is a gift that takes us beyond all our struggles, all our defenses, all our resistance and opens the door to go beyond all limitations and everything else that has kept us in pain and despair.

The gift of willingness does not require anything of us except a simple asking—we ask for God's Willingness to let go when we are still unwilling. We ask for the willingness to forgive when we are still caught up in hate and resentment. We ask for the willingness to see another way when we are still desperately trying to make things work our way. We ask for the willingness to pray in the midst of our doubts and fears. Willingness is given to us. This gift opens the door to receiving all other gifts. We are willing to see. We are willing to understand. We are willing to forgive. We are willing to let go. We are willing to be honest. We are willing to be guided. We are willing to be willing.

The gift of willingness is so precious, because it is the bridge that leads us from darkness into the light. It is a bridge that takes us beyond all doubt and fear and leads us to knowing. It is a bridge that reaches into our despair and shows us a choice of another way. It is the bridge between our solutions that have never worked, to the solutions God would give us.

The gift of willingness is all that is needed to accept all other gifts. If we are willing, we may be shown anything. If we are willing, we may be healed. If we are willing, we may be guided. If we are willing, we may be given and we may receive all gifts.

The gift of willingness is a beginning. We begin a life beyond denial, beyond disease, and beyond hopelessness. We begin to let God into our lives, for truly willingness is a gift of being reconnected with God.

With willingness we are teachable and we are reachable. With willingness there is nothing that cannot be healed.

Such a simple gift. Yet, the power of willingness is what will bring us Home.

"When I'm willing, I am able."

Prayer:

I still doubt, but I am willing to trust.

I am still afraid, but I am willing to see the Power of Love.

I still feel sick, but I am willing to find healing.

I am still holding on, but I am willing to let go.

I am still resentful, but I am willing to have forgiveness enter.

I am still confused, but I am willing to be given clarity.

I am still bound up in my beliefs, but I am willing to find freedom.

I still want to control, but I am willing to receive Your gifts beyond anything I would try to manage.

I still do not see my worth, but I am willing to be in touch with my completeness.

I still do not know how to find You—but I am willing...

--Amen

Being willing allows us to come from where we are and joins us with the possibility of all God precious gifts. We come without judgment; we come without expectations—we come with willingness.

THE GIFT OF WISDOM

We have not always been wise in making our decisions. We have not always been wise in what we have said or done. We have sought to change the world. We have sought to change others. But we have not looked at ourselves in true wisdom to say:

"This is where the change begins."

By ourselves we have very little wisdom, for true wisdom comes in being with our Higher Power. Our Higher Power is the Wisdom with which we will know ourselves. He is the wisdom with which we will recognize all wisdom: The wisdom there is in love and extending love. The wisdom there is in asking to see peace in each situation. The great wisdom there is in asking for honesty, in choosing honesty, whenever we speak, whenever we admit. The wisdom of forgiving and asking for forgiveness instead of continuing to be resentful. The wisdom of vulnerability and opening so true safety can be seen. The wisdom in being able to be and allowing others that freedom. The wisdom of accepting God's Will for us. The tremendous wisdom of beginning with gratitude for all we have and will be given.

The great wisdom of each gift is ours. The wisdom of gentleness instead of condemnation. The wisdom of God's Ease instead of our incessant struggles. The wisdom of beginning with ourselves in looking for whatever needs to be changed in the world. The wisdom of God's difference that teaches oneness instead of separation. The great wisdom of love that dissolves all hatred; that resolves all conflict and all fear.

True wisdom is the gift of our Higher Power showing us these gifts and their value. The wisdom of knowing our Higher Power's Will is the greatest wisdom that will bring all these gifts to us.

We are given the wisdom to choose healing instead of attack.

We are given the wisdom to choose release instead of holding on to our grievances.

We are given the wisdom to see innocence instead of judgment.

We are given the wisdom to let go of, instead of holding on to, the past.

We are given the wisdom to see our worth instead of the gift of ourselves that we have tried to throw away.

We are given the wisdom to see wholeness and inclusion instead of our blindness of separation.

We are given the wisdom of gifts.

We are given the wisdom of knowing these gifts are in each one of us.

We are given the wisdom of knowing ourselves.

We are given the wisdom of our Higher Power.

THE GIFT OF WONDER

The gift of Wonder is the gift of our true innocence.

The gift of Wonder is seeing everything with the eyes of a child.

The gift of Wonder is the ability to see everything in the freshness and newness of the moment.

The gift of Wonder sees others for the very first time without judgment.

The gift of Wonder is the consideration that there may be another way.

The gift of Wonder is the gift of total delight in each gift we receive and each gift we give.

The gift of Wonder is the total amazement we feel, watching the power of love heal each situation.

The gift of Wonder opens us to consider what gifts our Higher Power will bring today.

The gift of Wonder helps us to live in continual gratitude.

Life is full of wonder. With the gift of wonder, all prejudice is seen beyond, and we find each other. We are given the gift of Wonder for the beauty of our own inner being. We are given the gift of Wonder for the beauty of each other and the gifts we have to offer.

There is wonder in realizing—we are all entitled to so much. The gift of Wonder brings us in touch with the gift of humility—that in all humility, we are totally overwhelmed by the tremendous love that is all around us.

We are full of the wonder of love.

We are full of the wonder of beauty.

We are full of the wonder of each moment.

We are full of the wonder of joy.

We are full of the wonder of a power that loves us so much and gives us the gift of wonder.

We are full of wonder of the power, the divinity, within us.

We are full of awe at the wonder of God's Grace.

Each gift of wonder is one more connection with our oneness. Each gift of wonder is one more insight into the connectedness of all things.

The gift of Wonder places us in touch with the simplicity of asking, with the simplicity of our Higher Power's Will, with the miracle of all His solutions.

THE GIFT OF WORTH

We have tried to do many things in order to prove our worth—but we have not seen our completeness. Always has our worth seemed something or someone outside of ourselves and always when we have searched for it, we have failed to find it.

Truly, our worth is a gift. It is the gift we already have because it is a gift our Higher Power has already given us.

The gift of Worth puts us in touch with our completeness within. We are worthy in our Higher Power. Being with our Higher Power gives us all the worth we have to give.

The gift of Worth is the realization that our being encompasses everything. Our being is loving, is wise, is all-knowing, is connected, is worthy.

The gift of Worth proclaims that we are indeed worthy of all the gifts that are given us. We are worthy because each of us is a child of God that is loved unconditionally simply for our being.

We do not have to prove our worth, it is a gift. We do not have to find our worth, it is held in trust for us by our Higher Power. With the gift of Worth, we start from our completeness and open to Life. With the gift of Worth, we enter relationships in completeness rather than lack.

With the gift of Worth, we express what we love to do from a sense that we deserve to express and share who we truly are. We deserve respect. We don't have to prove we deserve respect—with the gift of Worth, it is understood. We deserve love, happiness, joy, support... not because we have proved our worth, but simply because our being is worthy.

The gift of Worth ends our desperate search and begins a journey of joyous expression of our being. It begins the opening to all the gifts that are ours. We finally meet ourselves and see the worth that has always been there. Our Higher Power gives us the vision to see the worth of ourselves and others. We are shown we are all worthy of our Higher Power's constant care, of our Higher Power's unconditional love. Our Higher Power is our Worth, for in this oneness are we all worthy of the healing, of the support, that is our Worth.

CONTINUING TO ASK FOR GIFTS

THE GIFT STORE IS ALWAYS OPEN

We have asked you to look at many conclusions that have brought you pain and separation. We have asked you to look at beliefs that have kept God's gifts from you. We have asked you to consider letting go of these conclusions and beliefs so that they may be replaced with another way of seeing and feeling. We have asked you to turn these conclusions over to your Higher Power in exchange for all the Gifts He will give you.

You look at all your conclusions and conclude that, in order to have these gifts or receive them, you must first get rid of all your conclusions. You think we are telling you about a condition you must fulfill before you can have happiness and joy in your life.

We wish to inform you there is no condition on receiving God's gifts. You do not have to get rid of anything in order for these gifts to be given. These gifts are continually given. They don't stop because you have conditions or conclusions on them. Your conclusions only block the awareness of these gifts—the gifts never stop flowing. They are continual; they are unconditional. We only point out blocks to receiving the flow of God's gifts. We do not make healing a condition. We only bring to your awareness the possibility of letting in more and more gifts with the willingness to let go of more and more of your conclusions.

BEING IN THE PRESENT IS BEING WITH THE PRESENCE

Please give me the Gift of Your Day.
Please give me the Gift of Your Love,
So I may have that Love to give.
Please give me the Gift of Your Asking,
So I may know what it is I truly desire.
Please give me the Gift of Your Patience,
So that I may allow both myself and others to be.

Please give me the Gift of Your Connection,
So I may be with others today.
Please give me the Gift of Your Forgiveness,
So I may see Innocence in whatever disturbs me.
Please give me the Gift of Your Being,
So I may be with all Truth and Integrity.
Please give me the Gift of Your Honesty,
So I may come to know all Truth in Your Gentleness.

Please give me the Gift of Your Knowing,
So I may see only what is loving as real.
Please give me the Gift of Your Support,
So I may know the certainty of Your Direction.
Please give me the Gift of Humility,
So that I may remember to ask for Your Guidance.

Please give me the Gift of Trust,
So I may see the choice I have in all matters.

Please give me the Gift of Your Prayer,
So I may be part of Your eternal blessing each moment.

--Amen

THE BACKWORD

We know that most books begin with a foreword, but we feel it appropriate for us to admit how we have had everything backward. We thought gifts came from things, and we thought value came from what was outside of us. We thought our goals came first and choosing the Peace of God came last. We thought our gift was in what we were doing rather than in what we were being. We had everything backwards.

We came to see that with each gift was the Presence of God and that was the real value. We thought we had to earn rather than to simply ask for these gifts. We thought we had to manufacture rather than allowing these gifts to be given. We thought we had to prove rather than simply be willing to be, to accept. We had it backwards, but each gift puts what is really important into focus. With each gift, we come to see what is real, what is healing, and we are given the awareness of the Peace of God.

May God's gifts be foremost in your life.

Other Books by
Leanne & Maynard Dalderis

Watch for the following books by the same authors on Kindle and Amazon in the near future:

- **Askceptance**
- **Do You Have a Moment?**
- **Where is Your Worth?**
- **Opening to Healing**
- **Letting Go One Step at a Time**

For book purchases, general inquiries and seminar/workshop information, contact the publisher at:

Guideline Productions Inc.
Calgary, Alberta, Canada
e| dalderis@vitagenics.ca
w| www.livingwithguidance.ca

SEMINAR BOOKINGS
Leanne and Maynard are available to share this information through seminars, workshops and group evenings (Gift Nights). Contact Guideline Productions Inc. at dalderis@vitagenics.ca for more information.

Manufactured by Amazon.ca
Acheson, AB

33142051R00160